MW01172481

Covenant Partnership

Beyond the Courts of Heaven

The intent of Covenant:

Hebrews 6:17-19   Living and Breathing Translation.

17 When Father God Himself wants to demonstrate the absolute certainty of His crazy, outrageous promises, He chooses to cut covenant with a man. So He not only gives His Word, but then goes on to back it up with this very binding promise. Now it is impossible for God to lie, so His Word really should be enough. But He wants us to be absolutely thoroughly certain and totally convinced that He meant what He said and will do exactly what He promised.

18 So He gives us not just one, but two absolute certainties for us to set our hope on for those times when we would otherwise be running for our lives.

19 This hope is like an anchor for our hearts, our souls and spirits; it's dug in, rock solid. Follow the anchor chain and see it goes right into Heaven itself. Follow it and it takes you right to the very Holy of Holies, the Heavenly throne room, into the radiant Presence of our Father God, where Jesus entered to be our High Priest, as a forerunner for us all.

Covenant Partnership—Beyond the Courts of Heaven.
By Jim V. Edwards
Copyright © 2022 Jim V. Edwards

ISBN-13: 978-1536915426
ISBN-10: 1536915424
Kindle ASIN: B09TTQZN3D

Published by Edwards Family Publishing
Cover Design by Jim Edwards with photo assistance from
Ernst Meyer
Editor Lara Farrell

All Scripture, unless otherwise marked, is taken from *The
Holy Bible*, King James Version.

Scriptures marked NIV are taken from the Holy Bible, New
International Version,® NIV,® Copyright ©1973, 1978, 1984,
2011 by Biblica Inc.® Used by permission. All rights reserved
worldwide.

Scriptures marked ASV are taken from the American Standard
Version

Scriptures marked as The Passion Translation®
By Dr Brian Simmons
Published by Broadstreet Publishing Group, LLC

Scriptures marked as L & B Translation are taken from the
Living and Breathing Translation of the epistles, written by
Jim Edwards, and published by Edwards Family Publishing.
The details are given in the back pages of this volume.

Printed by CreateSpace, and Amazon.com Company.
Available from Amazon.com and other book stores.
Available on Kindle and other devices.

Published by Edwards Family Publishing:
www.landbreathingt.com
Contact landbreathingt@gmail.com

On Facebook   Edwards-Family-Publishing
https://tinyurl.com/facelandbt

Dedication

I dedicate this to E.W. Kenyon whose life, ministry, and teaching laid so much of the foundation that this book builds on.

Thank you, Heavenly Dad, for choosing to cut covenant with us. Thank You for recognising our difficulty at taking You at Your Word, and cutting covenant with us that we may have this re-assurance that you really do mean what You promise to us.

Thank you, Jesus, for going through with it on our behalf and demonstrating to us the heart of your Father.

Thank you Holy Spirit for revealing Daddy's love to us.

Covenant Partnership

Table of Contents:

Dedication iii

Acknowledgements 1

History 1

Foundations 2

Chapter 1 Why Covenant 9

Chapter 2 Conditional versus Unconditional Covenants 15

Chapter 3 Jesus cutting covenant on our behalf 16

Chapter 4 Our New Covenant 19

Chapter 5 Jesus' Covenant Prayer 32

Chapter 6 Covenant Promises 37

Chapter 7 Cutting Covenant 45

Chapter 8 Covenant Relationship 48

Chapter 9 Abraham as our Example 55

Chapter 10 Moses the Covenant Broker 63

Chapter 11 David, His Anointing and Goliath 76

Chapter 12 David's Honor and Respect for the Anointing 83

Chapter 13 Learn how to build yourself up in the Lord 89

Chapter 15 David the Worshipper 98

Chapter 16 Covenant Celebration 104

Chapter 17 Intimacy 106

Chapter 18 Psalm 139 108

Chapter 19 Covenant Partnership Responsibilities 111

Chapter 20 Your Covenant Partnership Role 115

Chapter 21 Seeming Impossibilities 119

Postscript 127

About the Author 130

Additional Books by the Author: 131

Acknowledgements

Firstly a very big thank you to Lara Farrell for your wonderfully helpful suggestions, attention to detail and invaluable assistance in turning a raw manuscript into a book.

The covid lockdowns have been a strange period for many of us. This has been the environment for much of the writing and completion of this book. My own isolation has been tough, so I would like to specifically thank Sue Louck and her friends, largely in Southern California, for their online bible study and prayer times. They have been so helpful and supportive. I highly recommend Sue and her husband Bud's YouTube videos on their 'Upper Room Chats' channel with very helpful teachings on relationships. We can all do with improving our relationships, the close ones and the not so close.

History

Roger Price was the one person who got me started on the significance of Covenant, closely followed by E.W. Kenyon and his wonderful little booklet 'The Blood Covenant', ISBN 13:978-1-57770-15-9. I came upon these many years ago, from which I wrote my earlier book, *Mercy – God's Covenant Assistance*. But the revelation contained here is much more recent and builds on that basic understanding. I have much appreciated Robert Henderson's teaching on the Courts of Heaven, but I quickly realized it didn't go far enough, and Covenant Partnership completes the picture.

Most of us have never been exposed to these Covenant concepts that were intrinsic in Old Covenant times. With such a poor comprehension of the covenant roots of the Last Supper, I have concluded that covenant was not a normal part of Greek culture, to which most New Covenant literature was addressed. The letter to the Hebrews is the one epistle that does cover covenant, so the inference is that Jewish culture had not completely forgotten its covenant roots. That covenant is never explained in the Gospels or other epistles illustrates how its significance was very largely lost on those early believers.

Foundations

Robert Henderson in his teaching on the Courts of Heaven has done a wonderful job of educating the Body of Christ in the dimensions of prayer and our relationship with our Heavenly Father. This book outlines yet another dimension that builds on the others. Just as Robert Henderson outlines, each dimension builds on the previous ones. This new dimension, similarly builds on the earlier ones.

In response to the request by the disciples to teach them to pray, Jesus first taught them to address God, the-Almighty-One as their 'Abba' which in Aramaic is our word Daddy. This is the most intimate, simple and basic of relationships: Luke 11:2. This is the first step we must take in our journey to know Him, to see Him, to relate to Him and to refer to Him as our 'Abba'—Daddy. This word is the infant's first word, their first name for their father, 'Abba'.

On receiving Jesus as our Lord and Saviour we are adopted into His family, with Jesus as our big brother, so it is natural that we should come to know His Father as our Daddy, Romans 8:15 and Galatians 4:6; Holy Spirit who we received on receiving Jesus, cries out from our hearts "Abba", Daddy, to Father God.

You may have heard it said that we are far too familiar with a God we hardly know. At first glance this sounds like the exact opposite of that previous paragraph, but there is a huge difference between intimacy and familiarity. Familiarity is just half a step away from arrogant presumption. Jesus is teaching us that this intimate dependency is the very route, the lens through which He has chosen for us to get to know Him. Matthew 18:3-5, "except ye become as little children, ye shall not enter the kingdom of heaven" (KJV). But this strikes deeply at our self-sufficiency, at our earthly maturity and wisdom. Intimacy is a two-way process, so we have to be open-hearted and pursue intimacy with Him, for Him to be intimate with us.

The corollary to this acknowledged dependency is, "Give us today our daily bread." So He delights that we ask Him for our daily needs, and trust in His provision to us of our basic needs. In Matthew 6:7 & 8 Jesus makes two additional points, firstly that we aren't to make vain repetitions as though we are more likely to be heard by us repeating ourselves. To keep repeating the same request is an expression of our unbelief in that He didn't hear us the first time! The second point is that our Heavenly Daddy knows what we need before we even get to ask Him—but that doesn't negate our need to ask Him, or His Joy at listening to our basic requests and seeing our simple trust in His provision.

But our relationship with our earthly father changes as we grow up. As we mature, more is expected of us. Consciously or unconsciously, deliberately or not, we are given more responsibility. That relationship grows as each comes to understand the other's nature, their desires and their ways. The son or daughter learns their father's ways, his demands and expectations, which become their own. So too— as we draw close to the God and Father of our Lord Jesus the Anointed One, we grow to understand His Heart and His Ways. Now in English, the infants' 'Daddy' morphs to 'Dad' for what they call their father as they grow up, and even to my adult children I am still their 'Dad'. This has a very different set of intimate and close connotations to 'Father'. Can we grow that relationship with our Heavenly Father, from that infant's intimacy and trust of 'Daddy', through to 'Dad'? My hope and prayer is that this book will help you to make that transition.

From this point forward I will be deliberately referring to our Heavenly Father as our Heavenly Dad, to underline this point and to help us make that transition. This doesn't make me comfortable, and it probably doesn't sit easily with you either. But this precisely makes this point as to just how far we are from the level of intimacy, into-me-you-see, that He is looking for from you and me. If one of my children called me 'Father' I would be seriously upset and disturbed as to what was going on in their heads!

But Jesus' teaching did not stop at Luke 11:2. In Luke 11:5-8 He then went on to describe a friend waking up a reluctant neighbour at midnight to provide bread for his visitor. This is a description of persistent, insistence to a friend, in an untimely situation. This was Jesus' illustration to another dimension or aspect of our relationship with our Heavenly Dad. This is similar to the relationship we have with our earthly dad, as a child's relationship grows into true respectful friendship. So it is appropriate for us to come to our Heavenly Dad, as His friend, on behalf of those who we have come to love. As we grow in our friendship with our Heavenly Dad, we grow in our understanding of what He loves to give, and what He will not give under any circumstances—and of course, everything in between. As we grow in that relationship, we learn the value He places on things, on relationships, on justice and so on. As we grow in our relationship, we learn what we can ask for, and how to ask for it.

It has been a wonderful privilege as a parent to watch my children grow from tiny tots to adulthood. They are all wonderfully different with very different careers, different dreams and aspirations. It has been my wife's and my role as parents to encourage and bring out their uniqueness within the framework of our family—what a role—what a privilege! As I see them each excel in their different innovative and creative careers and life, this is humbling and exciting and the best years are ahead for each of them. How much more does our Heavenly Dad delight over you and me!

He knows our strengths and our weaknesses. He knows our longings, our hopes and our fears, our traumas and feeble grasp on His saving Grace. He knows what He can entrust to us that we will take responsibility for, and what we can accomplish with His special help.

It is in this context Jesus taught his disciples to keep on asking, so that they would keep on receiving—Luke 11:9-13 —keep on seeking and you will keep on finding, keep on knocking and it will be opened up for you.... How much more will your Heavenly Dad give Holy Spirit to those who ask Him. Superficially this is the complete contradiction of His earlier teaching that we aren't to make vain repetitions as though we are more likely to be heard by us repeating ourselves, Matthew 6:7. But this is not praying over our needs. He longs to give us way more than our basic necessities. This is praying for what we desire—over and above our physical 'needs', these are our 'wants'. The way we pray, how much we pray, how passionately we pray for these, is a measure of just how much we want them, just how desperate we are, and how desperate we are to grow in this family-likeness.

At this point I would ask you the reader—how well do you know your Heavenly Dad? How intimate, how trusting, how mature is that relationship? I dare you to stop and think this through with Him. Maybe He is still your Heavenly Daddy and you are totally dependent on Him in every possible way, then rejoice in your helplessness and your total dependency on Him. You will not need me to tell you there is so much more, but do not despise your current dependency and childlike relationship with Him. It is hugely precious to Him and a step all too many have missed in their rush to try and grow up. Remember Jesus seriously rebuked His disciples for trying to prevent the little children from coming to Him, concluding that 'such is the Kingdom of God' Mark 10:14 and Luke 18:16.

Maybe you still see Him and relate to Him respectfully as your Heavenly Father with a respectful distance between you. This I love and respect, and while it seems to run counter to intimacy it is a counterpart to it. But... Maybe you need to come back and re-evaluate just what Jesus was teaching the disciples and how that should apply in your relationship with Him.

It isn't until chapter 18 in Luke's gospel that Jesus takes this relationship a significant step forward to see our Heavenly Dad as a just judge who will speedily give justice to those who come to Him persistently and faithfully presenting their cases to Him—Luke 18:8.

This has huge ramifications that Robert Henderson has wonderfully explored and presented to us[1]. Our adversary does

---

[1] Robert Henderson has written many books and there is much of his teaching on-line. The following are simply examples:

Operating in the Courts of Heaven
    By Robert Henderson ISBN:978-0-8998-5481-6
Unlocking Destinies from the Courts of Heaven
    By Robert Henderson ISBN:978-0-9772460-4-5
Receiving Healing from the Courts of Heaven
    By Robert Henderson ISBN:978-0-7684-1754-8
Introduction to the Courts of Heaven:
    www.youtube.com/watch?v=4Xk2UChVsB0
Robert Henderson Courts of Heaven:
    Session 1: www.youtube.com/watch?v=A-MANcuJwVo
    Session 2: www.youtube.com/watch?v=Ww4L1yjc5G0
    Session 3: www.youtube.com/watch?v=6bIv14RGkWg
    Session 4: www.youtube.com/watch?v=oNClG9EhwWA
    Session 5: www.youtube.com/watch?v=GOZ_VzrG_Yg
    Session 6: www.youtube.com/watch?v=6EBKeGC1LOo

everything he can to present legal cases against us to prevent us moving forward in our destinies, in our health, relationships, and ministry. Here our Dad is handing us the responsibility to put together a response to our adversary's accusations and legal cases against us and our blood line and bring them before Him as a wonderful just judge who will speedily bring His just judgment to His Chosen Ones.

I would very highly recommend that before going much further into this book, that you thoroughly familiarise yourself with Robert Henderson's view and understanding of the Courts of Heaven.

But there is more! Our Heavenly Father, our Heavenly Dad is a covenant making and covenant keeping God who longs to have Covenant Partners to bring His Kingdom to earth.

Our Heavenly Father, our Heavenly Dad, has always cut covenant with people. Throughout the Old Testament, covenants are clearly described. The shedding of blood is a key part of initiating a covenant, hence the reference to 'cutting' covenant rather than 'making' covenant, or 'entering into a covenant relationship'. So what does this bring to our relationship with our Heavenly Dad? And what does this bring to our lives?

There came a point in Abram's life outlined in Genesis chapter 15, when the Lord appeared to Abram and shared how He wanted to cut covenant with him. He wanted to bless Abram outrageously—outrageously more than Abram could believe for, but right on what was on Abram's heart, Genesis 15:1-7. In the following verses we have a wonderful procedure that would have mirrored two people cutting covenant—with the two parties walking between the carcasses together, except here only the Lord walks between them. This signifies an unconditional covenant—completely unconditional on Abram, Genesis 15:18.

Curiously the Lord comes back to Abram in Genesis 17:2 and declares that He will make a covenant between Him and Abram—almost as though Abram really didn't get it the first time around. So how many times do you and I need to reinforce that covenant relationship?

Genesis 17:2, & 4-8. Here's this man, now 99 years old whose wife is 89 and they still have no children, and here's Father God declaring He wants to bless them so wildly that his descendents will be nations across the earth, (vs 5). He wants to bring Abram and Sarai from laughing at Him, (Genesis 17:17, & 18:12) to match the description given in Hebrews 11:11, of examples to us of faith in Him. And He also promises to give them the whole of the land of Canaan for an everlasting possession.

Unlike Genesis Chapter 15, this covenant the Lord cut with Abram was conditional on Abram circumcising every male child, and included Abram and Sarai being given new names, Abraham and Sarah.

These two chapters give us wonderful illustrations of so many aspects of cutting covenant in ancient times, but the key is how they illustrate that principle outlined for us in Hebrews 6:18. The Lord's promises are so much greater than we would dare to ask or believe Him for.

But, as always, our New Covenant is so, so much better than the Old! (Hebrews 8:13)

Chapter 1   Why Covenant

When you cut covenant with someone—you enter into a deep, very legally binding relationship. So this builds on the legal framework and world of the courtroom.

This is usually entered into between two people because of the love and trust that have built up over time, such as the marriage covenant, between husband and wife. It places all of the resources of one partner at the disposal of the other. The friends of one become the friends of the other; similarly the enemies of one become the enemies of the other.

When you first gave your life to the Lord, you started that profound relationship with Him as your Heavenly Daddy. You started as a child, but there's a problem if 20 years on you are still in a similar relationship! My children have grown to adulthood and our relationships have similarly grown and matured through the years. They will forever be my children, but there's a level of friendship that has grown through those years. So while always recognizing I've been adopted into His Family as His Child, my relationship with my Heavenly Daddy has matured and grown through the years. So being in covenant partnership with the Lord in many ways builds on that relationship of friendship. It places all of God's resources at our disposal—but there is a cost to this!

All of our resources are equally available to Him.

Are you in?

You need to think it through pretty carefully before giving your agreement.

But this Covenant Partnership does not wait for our maturity. Adopted into the family, and still only spiritual babies, we are also brought into this covenant relationship. As our relationship grows, then so too should our understanding and recognition of this facet of the relationship. So too, the depths of what we can draw on will also grow.

The writer to the Hebrews in verse 6:18 gives us a very precious insight into our Heavenly Dad's purposes and perspective for cutting covenant with us. So it is good to spell these out at the outset. His purposes undergird covenant. He is fully conversant with our weakness and with who and what we are, and Covenant is a key way of addressing this.

Unfortunately, in most versions it is so condensed that we miss it. In *Living and Breathing Hebrews to Jude* I have quite deliberately expanded and amplified it somewhat, as I see it is so hugely important.

Hebrews 6:13-20   Living and Breathing Translation:

13 By way of illustration, when God wanted to make covenant promises to Abraham, He couldn't invoke a higher power or authority, 'cause there is none! His Word had to be His Bond when He said, "I'm going to bless you, bless you, and bless you some more. While right now you only have one son and heir, I'm going to multiply your descendants, and then multiply them again." And sure enough, Abraham was patient, maintaining his faith and trust that God would indeed do all that He said, and we can see today that this has indeed been amazingly fulfilled.

16 When two people cut covenant they do so before someone of higher authority, to hold them accountable. Often this will be with a priest invoking the cursing of their particular god or gods, should they break their covenant promises to each other. So when Father God Himself wants to demonstrate the absolute certainty of His crazy, outrageous promises, He chooses to cut covenant with a man. So He not

only gives His Word, but then goes on to back it up with this very binding promise. Now it is impossible for God to lie, so His Word really should be enough, but He wants us to be absolutely thoroughly certain and totally convinced that He meant what He said and will do exactly what He promised. So He gives us not just one, but two absolute certainties for us to set our hope on for those times when we would otherwise be running for our lives.

[19] This hope is like an anchor for our hearts, our souls and spirits; it's dug in, rock solid. Follow the anchor chain and see it goes right into Heaven itself. Follow it and it takes you right to the very Holy of Holies, the Heavenly throne room, into the radiant Presence of our Father God, where Jesus entered to be our High Priest, as a forerunner for us all. Under the auspices of a New Covenant, that fulfilled and superseded the Old Covenant, God declared Jesus a priest forever after the order of Melchizedek, and this priesthood was to be in the throne room of Heaven itself, not the man-made copy here in any temple on earth.

Our Heavenly Dad wanted to bless Abraham and Sarah way beyond what they could imagine. He had serious problems bringing them to see the magnitude of what He planned and purposed, let alone believe Him for it! When he mentioned it to them, Genesis 17:17, and Genesis 18:12, they each laughed at the absurdity! And don't kid yourself; you would too in their circumstances. Here's the rub—His plans are the same for you and I! So here are two things He has to do—He has to show you what He plans to do, and then He has to bring you to believing it, so you can then co-operate and co-labour with Him to see its fulfilment.

Our Heavenly Dad's promises to us are outrageous! They are way beyond what we would dare to ask or dream of, Ephesians 3:20. If His promises to you are not this big, then maybe you need to spend a little more time getting to know Him better, and getting to know His Word better too.

So if He wants to bless us so outrageously, then this gives Him a problem. Just how does He get us to believe Him? And we will need to believe Him if we are to pull these promises from Heaven, down into this world.

As He is God whose whole nature is absolutely just, right and always true and true to His Word, then His Word 'should' be enough. If He said it, then He meant it and that should be sufficient. It should be, but you and I have clay feet, and we all know just how impossible it is, when the impossible leers at us, staring us down.

So the writer to the Hebrews spells out our Heavenly Dad's solution: covenant. A covenant being legally binding, adds a whole additional dimension of 'security'—to use the bank-manager's term.

So we have our knowledge of our Heavenly Dad's nature and heart towards us—out of which comes 'His Word' to us. And we add on top of that, that we are in this legally binding agreement with Him which by definition covers all His promises to us. Because of this legality, we can go into the Courts of Heaven for those things that have been legally paid for by the Blood of Jesus, and assigned to you and I. And there we can ask the court to render the appropriate legal verdicts on our behalf.

Our Heavenly Dad's intent is then that we have this absolutely sure and certain faith in what He purposes to do. This is not presumption. Faith brings rest. So our Dad's intent is that these two absolute certainties put us in that precious place of restful faith in what He will do.

Now maybe you don't have a big imagination, but mine is pretty big. Either way, we probably need some help in perceiving something as huge as that which our Heavenly Dad wants to bless us with. So my trick question here is to ask people just where should we go to find what He wants to bless us with. [And to answer that you'll need to jump to Chapter 6.]

But there is one aspect I want to highlight here before we move on. The Lord, our Heavenly Dad, never ever takes anything away from us. To take things away is totally contrary to His nature. He loved us so much that He *gave* us His Son, Romans 8:32. "The gifts and calling of God are irrevocable," Romans 11:29 AMP. Now read that last quote again slowly... Everything God has given you is irrevocable... *everything*! So His Word confirms that He will never take it back. He will never take it back even if we try to give it back to Him! So what in our lives is not a gift from Him? Everything we have and are is a gift from Him, and He will never take it back— He's that generous! Is your picture of your Heavenly Dad someone desperately trying to get you to give everything to Him? i.e give your life and soul to Him? No way! He would like to help you use it wisely, but He doesn't want it back. It's yours to do with just as you choose. Now for me, that's one awesome responsibility!

He doesn't even take our sin away. Things would be so much simpler if He did. Jesus doesn't take our sin away, but as Isaiah put it, "He bore our sin" He bore its penalty upon Himself. He needs us to want to be free of it, and its hold on us, so badly that we run from it. That He doesn't take it away is one of the reasons why we find ourselves readily entangled and tripped up—see Galatians 5:1 and 2 Peter 2:20. When we are born again, He gives us His Spirit and His new life changes us from the inside so that sin loses its hold, but we have to choose to co-operate. He breaks sin's power and the

13

power of our addictions, but this is one reason why we so often need others' help to be fully free from them and their demonic roots.

He wrapped skin and bone around a dream of His, before the world was even formed—and in due time He gave you birth. He has a wonderful destiny ahead for you if you choose to accept it, but that is always your choice. Every step is your choice to make, or to refuse. And as you will see in later chapters this destiny is hugely bigger and greater than even your wildest dreams.

This is the nature of our Covenant Partner.
Romans 8:32:

> He that spared not his own Son, but delivered him up
> for us all, how shall He not with Him also freely give
> us all things? (KJV)

Does He want to take your deepest dreams and longings from you, and replace them with His? No, no, no and NO! Just dig a little deeper into what you really, really want in life, beyond scratching that itch that's shouting so loudly at you right now. That's hard to do for most of us. Give it time.

In the meantime, give your all into the situation you are currently in, or the opportunities in front of you. I'm sure David had no idea while he was taking care of those sheep on the hillside, as to where that would lead.

Chapter 2   Conditional versus Unconditional Covenants

Some of the promises made with Abram were completely unconditional. In particular, I reference here Genesis 15. In verse 12 it reads that Abram fell into a deep sleep while Father God, his Heavenly Dad, in the form of a smoking oven and flaming torch passed between the carcasses that Abram had laid out. Normally both parties would walk between the carcasses to confirm their part and agreement to it. So here his Heavenly Dad was making it abundantly clear to Abram in terms that he very clearly understood, that the fulfilment of that promise was totally unconditional on Abram's part. Now this promise looked most unlikely seeing as Abram and Sarai had no children. [See Genesis 15:18-21.]

But looking at very nearly all of the Old Testament promises they are prefixed with an 'if'. They are conditional promises. The covenant with Abram later, in Genesis 17:10 is prefixed by the requirement to circumcise their male infants as outlined in verse 11-14. The Mosaic covenant required the people to obey the Ten Commandments. This is the more typical nature of Old Testament promises.

But Jesus…! Jesus said He came "to fulfil all the Law and the Prophets", Matthew 5:17. So He fulfilled all of the terms and conditions of the Old Covenant promises on our behalf. So our failure to fully fulfil all of the terms and conditions of those promises no longer disqualifies us from asking, expecting, and receiving those promises. In most instances the conditions make perfect sense for the fulfilment of their respective promises. I am not suggesting that we should no longer make any attempt to comply fully with those conditions. The point I am trying to make here is that our failure to fulfil them *does not disqualify* us who are in Christ Jesus from believing for them, and receiving them.

Chapter 3 Jesus cutting covenant on our behalf

The accounts of the Last Supper in Matthew 26, Mark 14 & Luke 22 are all very similar.

Jesus set up the Passover celebration very carefully. I will draw on Luke's account as the most detailed and sensitive. Jesus set the Passover meal for Thursday evening, not the more usual Friday. This was quite normal if the Passover fell on a Sabbath, i.e. Friday evening, which this year it did. When this happened there was some flexibility as to which night the host would choose to celebrate it. Note that Jesus was crucified on the following day i.e. on the precise day that the Passover Lambs would have been slaughtered— such was the rush by the Jewish elders to have Jesus crucified and dead before the feast—the Passover, that started at sundown on Friday evening. [Note the instruction to see that all three of those crucified were dead before the beginning of the feast, John 19:31.]

But right at the start of the meal, Luke records for us the keenness and eagerness of Jesus to share this moment with His Disciples, Luke 22:15 "I have eagerly desired to eat this Passover with you before I suffer." Jesus must have celebrated Passover with His disciples in earlier years, but this was going to be different. In the middle of the very normal annual celebration of Passover He was going to initiate a completely New Covenant between man and our Father God. He was about to cut covenant with His Dad, offering His own Body as the covenant sacrifice to seal it.

My own belief is that at the Mount of Transfiguration when He met Moses and Elijah, that Moses revealed to Jesus (the man) the true nature and reality of Passover as a type, pointing to what Jesus would fulfil once and for all, on our behalf. The Lord was the One who had instructed Moses to initiate the Passover to protect the Hebrews so that the angel of death would pass over their houses in Egypt and save them from the plague. We will never know just how much Moses understood of the significance and meaning behind Passover, at the time he instigated it. As the person who saw it in Heaven and instigated it here, it would be appropriate that he is the one person to expound to Jesus, the man, just how He was to be the once and for all Passover sacrifice fulfilment for us all. It is notable that after this experience we have the comment that "Jesus set His Face to go to Jerusalem" Luke 9:51.

For a long time I have wondered at the significance of Elijah being there also. But very recently, while writing this book, I believe the Lord has shown me the reason. The sacrificial offering was only half of the story! This was to be followed by the Resurrection, which Elijah would have explained. Elijah was the first biblical character who had a recorded resurrection from the dead, so this would tie in. Jesus had to place Himself fully and entirely into the hands of His Father, His Dad, to raise Him back from the dead. There were two other highlights of Elijah's life to talk through with Jesus—his showdown with Baal and all that was against the Lord, and also his passing on his mantle to Elisha. Jesus fulfilled, both of these only on a cosmic scale, Matthew 28:18.

John adds another detail missing from the other Gospel accounts, of Jesus washing His disciples' feet. John even notes here in Chapter 13:1 & 3 that Jesus deliberately did this knowing that his hour had come to leave this world, and that everything had been given to Him. This is His Nature and our nature as a Covenant Partner with Him, to serve our fellow brothers and sisters.

So Jesus twists the normal wording of the Passover ritual only ever so slightly for both the bread and the wine. First He takes the bread. This would have been when the disciples have drunk the second cup and they are all then expectantly waiting for the host to offer the unleavened bread with the words, "This is the body of the Passover." Instead He says "This is *My* body." And as its sacrificial fulfilment, of course His is the body of the Passover.

The Passover meal finishes with the third cup, the *Cos ha-berachah*—the Cup of Blessing, as it was called. It is likely that it was this cup that Jesus passed round with those words that are now so familiar to us all, "This is *My* Blood of the New Covenant, do this as often as you drink it, in remembrance of Me." Here Jesus is entering into a covenant relationship with His Heavenly Dad on our behalf. He then goes on to offer Himself as the covenant's sacrificial offering to seal it. In His Wording, He requests that we continue to do this in His remembrance. So here, we are re-enacting the inauguration of this New Covenant. In remembering Him, we are signing up our agreement to this New Covenant. We are in effect saying this Covenant now exists between me and His Heavenly Dad, i.e. our Heavenly Dad, as a covenant passes down the generations.

So all of our Heavenly Dad's resources are now available to us as His Covenant Partner, and all of our resources are available to Him as our Covenant Partner.

Our Covenant Partner is our Heavenly Dad.

Chapter 4   Our New Covenant

Jesus cut covenant with Father God, His Heavenly Dad, on our behalf, at the last supper, and sealed it with the covenant sacrifice of Himself at Calvary. Having broken and shared the bread and the wine at their appropriate places in the Passover celebration, He then went on to teach His Disciples what being a Covenant Partner was going to look like. As John never includes the Passover Meal in his description of the Last Supper, it is easy to miss that Chapters 14 through 16 is Jesus teaching as to what being a Covenant Partner was going to look like. This is completely different to all of Jesus' earlier teaching on prayer. He then follows this by praying for them in Chapter 17, from His Standpoint of being in Covenant Partnership with His Heavenly Dad.

To keep referring to our 'Heavenly Dad', rather than our 'Father God' throughout this chapter especially, is a sharp, pointed reminder to me of the intimacy and nature of the relationship to which we are called. I have re-worded it this way quite deliberately, as I didn't initially write it this way, but Lara, my editor, had to point it out and remind me! Yes, I am still learning to embrace such intimacy and it is curious how our normal choice of words so readily betrays our inner world. Fortunately, by reframing our words, we help that process of reframing our inner world. And what could possibly be more important than that inner relationship with the "All Mighty One" and to align ourselves to the relationship Jesus taught us and modelled for us so perfectly.

So what did Jesus teach them in those three chapters? I here wanted to quote Jesus' words directly. While I would normally have chosen the KJV, the archaic language cuts right across the intimacy of these moments, so I have instead quoted directly from the NIV. In keeping with the rest of this book, I have capitalized where Jesus is referring to Himself, or addressing His Father, His Daddy, directly in prayer as 'You'.

John Chapter 14:

1/ John 14:1-4: There is now no place for fear for any possible reason. Fear of death is the ultimate fear, so Jesus addresses the fear of death first, head-on. He repeats this in verse 27. As His Covenant Partner we have all of His resources available to us to counter whatever it is that would make us afraid or fearful.

> [1] Let not your hearts be troubled: you believe in God, believe also in Me. [2] My Father's house has many rooms: if it were not so, would I have told you that I am going there to prepare a place for you? [3] And if I go and prepare a place for you, I will come back again, and take you to be with Me that you also may be where I am. [4] You know the way to the place where I am going. (NIV)

In response to Thomas' question in verse 5 that the disciples had absolutely no idea where Jesus was about to go, Jesus tells them, and us, the way to where He was headed. Curiously for some, He gives the route, not the destination. More succinctly than I could put it, Jesus is here spelling out the very intent of this book. To know Jesus, is to know His Dad. Jesus perfectly represented His Dad during His time here, and our resurrected Jesus continues to perfectly represent His Dad as they are One.

2/ John 14:6 & 7:

Jesus underlines the Oneness, between Himself and His Heavenly Dad in Verse 7, by telling them that they will come to realize that they have seen and experienced their Heavenly Dad, in their experience of Jesus:

⁶ Jesus answered, "I am the way and the truth and the life. No one comes to the Father except through Me. ⁷ If you really know Me, you will know My Father as well. From now on, you do know Him and have seen Him.

To which Philip said, "Lord, show us the Father and that will be enough for us," verse 8. In response to Philip, Jesus spells it out for them (and us!) 9-11:

⁹ Jesus answered: "Don't you know Me, Philip, even after I have been among you such a long time? Anyone who has seen Me has seen the Father. How can you say, 'Show us the Father'? ¹⁰ Don't you believe that I am in the Father, and that the Father is in Me? The words I say to you I do not speak on My own authority. Rather, it is the Father, living in Me, who is doing his work. ¹¹ Believe Me when I say that I am in the Father and the Father is in Me; or at least believe on the evidence of the works themselves. (NIV)

3/ John 14:12: Jesus spells out that those who believe in Him will do greater works than He did. Being raised to the level of Covenant Partner with the Father, Jesus' Heavenly Dad, takes us up to the same level of relationship with Him as Jesus enjoyed during His time here on earth. Stop and think about that for a moment—it sounds outrageous—horribly blasphemous, but this is the reality. These are Jesus' words:

¹² Very truly I tell you, whoever believes in Me will do the works I have been doing, and they will do even greater things than these, because I am going to the Father. (NIV)

4/ John 14:13: Whatever you ask in Jesus name, He will do it so that the Father will be glorified in the Son. He repeats this in verse 14, for emphasis—He means it!

> 13 And I will do whatever you ask in My Name, so that the Father may be glorified in the Son. 14 You may ask Me for anything in My Name, and I will do it. (NIV)

See just how different this is to Jesus' teaching in Luke 11:5-9, "ask and keep on asking…" Different situations require different ways to pray. Some things, especially our dreams and visions require us to keep on asking. But some things, especially major promises to us as individuals, or to us as intercessors in whatever sphere our remit is, we need to bring to the Lord as His Covenant Partner. We ask Him to do what He has to do—on the basis of that very legally binding Covenant Partnership that exists between Him and us.

5/ John 14:15-31: Jesus promises us Holy Spirit, to those who love Him, to help us and be with us forever—we aren't expected to do this alone! He has the role of advocate for us in the Courts of Heaven, but He is to be far more than 'with us' but comes to live 'in us'.

> 15 If you love Me, keep My commands. 16 And I will ask the Father, and He will give you another Advocate, to help you and be with you forever— 17 the Spirit of Truth. The world cannot accept Him, because it neither sees Him nor knows Him. But you know Him, for He lives with you and will be in you. (NIV)

Verses 18-20 add an extra twist to this. Jesus sums this up in verse 20 by here saying we will realize that He is in the Father—that we are in Him, and He is in us. This wonderfully portrays how each member of the Trinity is so similar to the others—so what is Holy Spirit like? —all but indistinguishable from Jesus!

> [18] I will not leave you as orphans; I will come to you. [19] Before long, the world will not see Me anymore, but you will see Me. Because I live, you also will live. (NIV)

What is Father like? "If you have seen Me, then you have seen the Father", John 14:9 was Jesus' definitive statement, but He adds extra detail here in verse 20:

> [20] On that day you will realize that I am in My Father, and you are in Me, and I am in you. (NIV)

Jesus then went on to spell out our response:

> [21] Whoever has My commands and keeps them is the one who loves Me. The one who loves Me will be loved by My Father, and I too will love them and show Myself to them. (NIV)

In response to Philip's question in verse 22, Jesus reinforces this with re-iterating Father's response:

> [23] Anyone who loves Me will obey My teaching. My Father will love them, and We will come to them and make our home with them. (NIV)

Jesus then goes on to tell us very specifically what Holy Spirit will do; that He will teach us all things, and remind the apostles of everything Jesus had said to them:

> [26] But the Advocate, the Holy Spirit, whom the Father will send in My Name, will remind you of everything I have said to you. (NIV)

Jesus completes this section by highlighting His intent and purpose behind what He has been trying to convey to them all, and to us too, as we read them—Peace! Shalom! [Nothing missing, nothing broken!]

> [27] Peace I leave with you, My Peace I give you. I do not give to you as the world gives. Do not let your hearts be troubled, and do not be afraid.

> [28] You heard Me say, 'I am going away and I am coming back to you.' If you loved Me, you would be glad that I am going to the Father, for the Father is greater than I. (NIV)

John Chapter 15:

6/ John 15:1-8: The Vine and the branches and the importance of staying in the vine, into which we have been grafted. The relationship into which we are brought when we enter into a relationship with the Lord, enables us to bear fruit for Him:

> [1] I am the True Vine, and My Father is the gardener.
> [2] He cuts off every branch in Me that bears no fruit, while every branch that does bear fruit He prunes so that it will be even more fruitful. [3] You are already clean because of the word I have spoken to you. (NIV)

In verse 4 we are called to be grafted into His Vine so that His Life can flow into us. The Passion Translation® calls this 'life-union'. This is Covenant Partnership—it is so much more than simply abiding! While we are in Him then He tends and cares for us, pruning us, lifting and cleaning us up like a good vinedresser, so that we bear good fruit. But without that we will be like a branch that is thrown into the fire and burned—Verse 6. It is in this context that Jesus once again says, "If you remain in Me and My words remain in you, ask what you wish, and it will be done for you. This is to My Dad's glory, that you bear much fruit," in verses 7 & 8.

> 4 Remain in Me, as I also remain in you. No branch can bear fruit by itself; it must remain in the vine. Neither can you bear fruit unless you remain in Me.
> 5 I am the vine; you are the branches. If you remain in Me and I in you, you will bear much fruit; apart from Me you can do nothing. 6 If you do not remain in Me, you are like a branch that is thrown away and withers; such branches are picked up, thrown into the fire and burned.
> 7 If you remain in Me and My Words remain in you, ask whatever you wish, and it will be done for you.
> 8 This is to My Father's glory, that you bear much fruit; showing yourselves to be My disciples. (NIV)

7/ John 15:9-14, & 17: Friendship with Him, and each other:

There is a natural corollary to this that we stay in love with Him, and the corollary to that is we stay in love with other believers, laying our lives down for them. And this takes us to a whole new level in our relationship with Him.

> 9 As the Father has loved Me, so I have loved you. Now remain in My Love. 10 If you keep My commands you will remain in my love, just as I have kept My Father's commands and remain in his love.
> 11 I have told you this so that My Joy may be in you and that your joy may be complete. 12 My Command is this: love each other as I have loved you. 13 Greater love has no one than this, to lay down one's life for one's friends. 14 You are My Friends if you do what I command. (NIV)

Covenant Partnership

John 15:15-16: Friendship with Him:

> ¹⁵ I no longer call you servants, because a bond-servant [slave] does not know his master's business. Instead, I have called you friends, for everything that I learned from My Father I have made known to you. ¹⁶ You did not choose Me, but I chose you and appointed you so that you might go and bear much fruit—fruit that will last—and so that whatever you ask in My Name My Dad will give you. (NIV)

8/ John 15:18-25: Disciples hated by the world:

> ¹⁸ If the world hates you, keep in mind that it hated Me first. ¹⁹ If you belonged to the world, it would love you as its own. As it is, you do not belong to the world, but I have chosen you out of the world. That is why the world hates you. ²⁰ Remember what I told you: 'A servant is not greater than his master.' If they persecuted Me, they will persecute you also. If they obeyed My teaching, they will obey yours also.

9/ John 15:26-27: Jesus here gives us a very succinct description of the work of Holy Spirit, in us and through us:

> ²⁶ When the Advocate comes, whom I will send to you from the Father—the Spirit of Truth who goes out from the Father—He will testify about Me. Holy Spirit of Truth will testify of Me (Jesus). ²⁷ And 'you also must testify, for you have been with Me from the beginning'. (NIV)

So both Holy Spirit and believers, with His Anointing, co-working with Him will testify of Jesus. This is a very legal term—will give legal evidence—description and proof of Jesus' resurrection—of His Lordship over everything, and His selfless nature of forgiveness and love.

John Chapter 16:

10/ John 16:1-4: The inevitability of persecution by those who don't know the Lord:

> [1] All this I have told you so that you will not fall away. [2] They will put you out of the synagogue; in fact, the time is coming when anyone who kills you will think they are offering a service to God. [3] They will do such things because they have not known the Father or Me. [4] I have told you this, so that when their time comes you will remember that I warned you about them. I did not tell you this from the beginning because I was with you. (NIV)

11/ John 16:5-7: Jesus tells them He is going back to Heaven, but He has to return there if He is to send Holy Spirit:

> [5] but now I am going to Him who sent Me. None of you asks Me, 'Where are you going?' [6] Rather, you are filled with grief because I have said these things. [7] But very truly I tell you, it is for your good that I am going away. Unless I go away, the Advocate will not come to you; but if I go, I will send Him to you. (NIV)

12/ John 16:8-15: Next Jesus lists the work of Holy Spirit:

Vs 8. He will expose sin and reveal how wrong people's perception is of our Heavenly Dad's righteousness and judgments:

> [8] When He comes, He will prove the world to be in the wrong about sin and righteousness and judgment. (NIV)

Vs 9 He will expose sin in those who refuse to believe that Jesus is Lord of all:

> [9] about sin, because people do not believe in Me; (NIV)

Vs 10 He will expose righteousness because Jesus returned to His Dad:

> [10] about righteousness, because I am going to the Father, where you can see Me no longer; (NIV)

Vs 11 He will bring judgment because the prince of this world has been judged:

> [11] and about judgment, because the prince of this world now stands condemned. (NIV)

Vs 13 He will guide us into all truth, by telling us what our Heavenly Dad is saying and doing:

> [13] But when He, the Spirit of Truth, comes, He will guide you into all the truth. He will not speak on His own; He will speak only what He hears, and He will tell you what is yet to come. (NIV)

Vs 14 &15 He will glorify Jesus by revealing His power and glory and reveal it to us, together with all that our Heavenly Dad has that He has given to Jesus:

> [14] He will glorify Me because it is from Me that He will receive what He will make known to you. [15] All that belongs to the Father is mine. That is why I said the Spirit will receive from Me what He will make known to you. (NIV)

Yes! *Everything* our Heavenly Dad has, He has given to Jesus! That's what Jesus is saying here!

13/ John 16:16-22: The conundrum of the pain and grief of Jesus returning to His Heavenly Dad and leaving the disciples, and their joy at His returning:

> [16] Jesus went on to say, "In a little while you will see Me no more, and then after a little while you will see Me."
>
> [17] At this, some of his disciples said to one another, "What does He mean by saying, 'In a little while you will see Me no more, and then after a little while you will see Me,' and 'Because I am going to the Father'?" [18] They kept asking, "What does He mean by 'a little while'? We don't understand what He is saying."
>
> [19] Jesus saw that they wanted to ask Him about this, so He said to them, "Are you asking one another what I meant when I said, 'In a little while you will see Me no more, and then after a little while you will see Me'? [20] Very truly I tell you, you will weep and mourn while the world rejoices. You will grieve, but your grief will turn to joy. [21] A woman giving birth to a child has pain because her time has come; but when her baby is born she forgets the anguish because of her joy that a child is born into the world. [22] So with you: Now is your time of grief, but I will see you again and you will rejoice, and no one will take away your joy. (NIV)

And with this, Jesus introduces us to His Heavenly Dad and explores the relationship He expects His Disciples to have with Him.

14/ John 16:23 & 24: We won't need to ask Jesus for anything, but because of our relationship with Him, we will go straight to our Heavenly Daddy "and whatsoever you will ask your Heavenly Daddy in Jesus' name, He will give it to you. So far you have asked for nothing in My Name. Ask, and keep on asking and you will keep on receiving; that your joy may be full."

> [23] In that day you will no longer ask Me anything. Very truly I tell you, My Father will give you whatever you ask in My Name. [24] Until now you have not asked for anything in My Name. Ask and you will receive, and your joy will be complete. (NIV)

Whatsoever you ask for! This pre-supposes that we are in such an intimate relationship that our requests mirror what He purposes, 1 John 3:22, 1 John 5:15.

15/ John 16:25-26: We won't ask Jesus to ask our Heavenly Dad, but because of our relationship with Jesus, we will go directly to our Heavenly Dad and ask 'in His Name':

> [25] "Though I have been speaking figuratively, a time is coming when I will no longer use this kind of language but will tell you plainly about My Father. [26] In that day you will ask in My Name. I am not saying that I will ask the Father on your behalf. (NIV)

16/ John 16:27: for our Heavenly Dad loves us because of our love for Jesus and because we believe that Jesus came from our Heavenly Dad:

> [27] No, the Father himself loves you because you have loved Me and have believed that I came from God. (NIV)

17/ John 16:32: The disciples would be scattered, leaving Jesus all alone, but with our Heavenly Dad:

> [32] A time is coming and in fact has come when you will be scattered, each to your own home. You will leave Me all alone. Yet I am not alone, for My Father is with Me. (NIV)

The overall conclusion:

18/ John 16:33: Jesus has shared these truths so that we may have His Peace, regardless of our circumstances. "In the world you will have tribulation: but be of good cheer; I have overcome the world."

> [33] I have told you these things, so that in Me you may have peace. In this world you will have trouble. But take heart! I have overcome the world. (NIV)

We need to combine these different aspects. We stand before our Covenant Partner, God Himself, with all of His unlimited resources, but combine this with the other concepts that Jesus taught us. He is our Daddy! He is our best friend! He gives us Holy Spirit to come and live in us—the very same Spirit who lived in Jesus, 1 Corinthians 3:16. This is the One who invites us into this relationship of Covenant Partnership.

He is the great Just Judge to render justice and mercy on behalf of His children.

Chapter 5   Jesus' Covenant Prayer

Having spelled out so much of what this covenant relationship with Our Heavenly Dad was going to look like, John then records for us Jesus' prayer for us in John Chapter 17.

For the first eight verses Jesus is affirming His relationship with His Heavenly Dad and the unity they enjoyed before the universe was even created (vs 5):

> [1] After Jesus said this, he looked toward heaven and prayed:
> "Father, the hour has come. Glorify Your Son, that Your Son may glorify You. [2] For You granted Him authority over all people that He might give eternal life to all those You have given Him. [3] Now this is eternal life: that they know You, the only true God, and Jesus Christ, whom You have sent. [4] I have brought You glory on earth by finishing the work You gave Me to do. [5] And now, Father, glorify Me in Your presence with the glory I had with You before the world began.
> [6] "I have revealed You to those whom You gave Me out of the world. They were Yours; You gave them to Me and they have obeyed Your word. [7] Now they know that everything You have given Me comes from You. [8] For I gave them the words You gave Me and they accepted them. They knew with certainty that I came from You, and they believed that You sent Me. (NIV)

Then Jesus moves on to praying for His Disciples. Note here the reciprocity in their relationship to which we are similarly called, in verse 10:

[9] I pray for them. I am not praying for the world, but for those You have given Me, for they are Yours. [10] All I have is Yours, and all You have is Mine. And glory has come to Me through them. [11] I will remain in the world no longer, but they are still in the world, and I am coming to You. Holy Father, protect them by the power of Your Name, the Name You gave Me, so that they may be one as We are one. [12] While I was with them, I protected them and kept them safe by that Name You gave Me. (NIV)

He clearly knows just what lay ahead (vs 11 & later in vs 24). This is in stark contrast with the situation described in Chapter 10 of John's Gospel.

In Chapter 10, only a very short time before Passover and this prayer, after a bruising encounter with the Jewish Leaders arguing precisely over His identity, Jesus left and went back to where John had been baptising. He went back to the place of His baptism where His Heavenly Dad had spoken over Him, "This is my beloved Son in whom I'm well pleased." And even when called to come and pray for Lazarus by some of his closest friends He stays there and doesn't move. It is as though He is staying in this place until that Word has fully taken root once more.

Back to Jesus prayer of Chapter 17, He now starts praying for His disciples and all who belong to Him and His Heavenly Dad, and for us too who believe in Jesus through their testimony (vs 20):

[13] "I am coming to You now, but I say these things while I am still in the world, so that they may have the full measure of My Joy within them. [14] I have given them Your Word and the world has hated them, for they are not of the world any more than I

am of the world. [15] My prayer is not that You take them out of the world but that You protect them from the evil one. [16] They are not of the world, even as I am not of it. [17] Sanctify them by the truth; Your Word is truth. [18] As You sent Me into the world, I have sent them into the world. [19] For them I sanctify Myself, that they too may be truly sanctified.
[20] "My prayer is not for them alone. I pray also for those who will believe in Me through their message. (NIV)

So you and I are included quite specifically in Jesus' prayer here. So what is He praying for us? His biggest concerns are our protection and our unity; that He mentioned in verse 11. In verses 21-23 He expands in these. He prays that we experience and live out the same unity that He enjoys with His Heavenly Dad:

[21] that all of them may be one, Father, just as You are in Me and I am in You. May they also be in Us so that the world may believe that You have sent Me. [22] I have given them the glory that You gave Me, that they may be one as We are one— [23] I in them and You in Me—so that they may be brought to complete unity. Then the world will know that You sent Me and have loved them even as You have loved Me. (NIV)

So what does this unity look like and how does it work itself out? Jesus and the Father are clearly different, just as we are all very different, so this unity is clearly not clonish conformity! The unity that Jesus has with His Heavenly Dad is a unity of Spirit and Purpose—a unity of heart and intent. He goes on to qualify this in vs 23 that we will experience perfect unity because we will have Jesus Himself living in us.

34

He goes on to pray that we experience Father's endless love just as He had experienced, as He prays for this love to come and live in us, in verse 26, because He is living in us:

> [24] "Father, I want those You have given Me to be with Me where I am, and to see My glory, the glory You have given Me because You loved Me before the creation of the world.
>
> [25] "Righteous Father, though the world does not know You, I know You, and they know that You have sent Me. [26] I have made You known to them, and will continue to make You known in order that the love You have for Me may be in them and that I Myself may be in them." (NIV)

Oh how important it is that we each *experience* Him coming and living in us. Our Christian life is so much more than believing a creed! It is a walk of day by day experiencing the Spirit of Jesus living in us! This was Jesus' heart and prayer for us. See Romans 8:9:

> You are learning how to live out that 'Law of Life' with Holy Spirit, with Him growing more and more in your hearts, in your minds and in your bodies. If you don't have Holy Spirit living in you, then don't try and kid yourself; try all you might, you really aren't a Christian.   *L and B Translation*

Jesus expects this to be so powerfully visible and visibly different to how other people live and operate that this becomes proof that our Heavenly Dad did indeed send Jesus to be our Passover sacrifice and Saviour (vs 23).

This harks back to Psalm 133:

Behold how good and pleasant it is for brethren to dwell together in unity... It is in this atmosphere that He *commands* the blessing, even life for evermore.

> *Oh,* my Wonderful King Jesus, it's so good, so sweet when my heart and Your heart beat together as one. May that same sweet fragrance of unity spill over to all those who also know and love You. You do something so, so special when we finally put aside our differences and crown You King Jesus as our Lord and our King, and join in the same unity You, Papa and Holy Spirit enjoy.

> *Oh,* Your anointing flowing down, Holy Spirit, is like thick anointing oil running over our faces and beards, down our shirts and clothes right down to our feet—*Oh,* how much we need that—how precious, how special it is! *Oh,* what a fragrance! It's like the dew on Mount Hermon that gathers and flows down in joyful rivulets watering a parched and weary land. It's like the dew of Heaven watering parched and weary spirits!

> *Oh* Jesus, bring it on—for it's here You command the blessing—it's here You bring Healing, Joy, Refreshing, and LIFE. And, Lord, because that's the way You are—thank You that it's always like that, because You are like that.

> More, Lord! More!
> *Psalm 133 Living and Breathing the Psalms*

Chapter 6   Covenant Promises

So where do we go to find what our Heavenly Dad has promised to us? As Christians we naturally look to the New Testament, and this is certainly full of some wonderful promises. Many push these out to another epoch, rather than pressing in with our relationship with our Heavenly Dad to see them brought into today. But David, who I look at a lot more closely in later chapters, somehow entered into a relationship very much like our New Covenant one, a 1000 years before Jesus was born! While he was never a priest He had an intimate and prophetic relationship with the Lord, as a Covenant Partner. And it was David's Tent of worship that was to set the example for New Covenant worship, as prophesied by Amos:

> "After this I will return and rebuild David's fallen tent. Its ruins I will rebuild and I will restore it, that the rest of mankind may seek the Lord, even all the Gentiles who bear my name, says the Lord, who does these things—things known from long ago," Acts 15:16-18, quoting Amos 9. (NIV)

This was quoted by James at the first Jerusalem Council concluding their discussion concerning the whole nature of the New Covenant Church full of believers who weren't of Jewish origin.

So if David pulled the future into his day, then so we should pull those promises into today, rather than push them out to some later epoch. It is our responsibility to pull that epoch into today.

So the other, very natural place we can look for covenant promises is in the Old Testament. There is a somewhat curious facet of Old Testament scripture. The

Sadducees of Jesus' time did not believe in any life after death, in spite of every book in the Old Testament being there for them. When they raised this with Jesus, His answer appears to us to be remarkably oblique for such a huge and specific issue. The same answer is recorded for us in Matthew 22:32, Mark 12:26, and Luke 20:37 that when God was talking to Moses from the burning bush, He referred to Himself, saying, "I *am* the God of Abraham, Isaac and Jacob," inferring that these are all still living.

So all of the promises there in the Old Testament are clearly for here and now on planet earth—not for the millennium and certainly not for our lives in Heaven after we have left here. Yes, there is life for us there in Heaven when we leave here and there are promises given to us by Jesus and others there in the New Testament that apply to our life there, such as Jesus' promise to us in John 14:2, that in His Heavenly Dad's house there are many mansions prepared for us to live in. But all those Old Covenant promises are for here and now on planet Earth!

So our Bible is a wonderful place to go for our Heavenly Dad's precious promises to us, with the added advantage that these are clearly written down for us, with a measure of security that they have survived the test of time with many confirming their validity for us. As Paul set out for us in 2 Timothy 3:16,

> Every one of those scriptures was written by Holy Spirit, whoever's name it goes by.
>
> *L & B Translation*

And if He has written it, then we can indeed take those promises as our Heavenly Dad's Word to us—as the very personal word of our Heavenly Dad to us.

But our Bible is not the only source of our Heavenly Dad's promises to us! Holy Spirit is alive and well and living within us, and He brings us and opens up to us promises specific to us. He also provides prophets within the Body of Christ who often bring His promises to us. With these it is pretty essential that we set these down so we can return to them often and keep them to mind. It is all too easy when the going gets tough, or long, to forget the promise that set us off in the first place, or forget the details. Paul writes to Timothy to,

> Remember and hold fast to the prophecies spoken over you and given to you. These words, these promises from Father God, from our Heavenly Dad, with faith and a clear conscience, are mighty spiritual weapons. These are key personal weapons for your warfare against those forces and all that comes against you,   1 Timothy 1:18
>
> *L and B Translation*

Those details are so important and easy to forget. Now many of those biblical promises include detail that may well have made little to no sense to the person setting it down, but makes wonderful sense in hindsight, as we look back at their fulfilment.

But with all that said, there is one chapter in the Torah that spells out a wonderful collection of very practical and specific covenant promises, Deuteronomy 28. Now these are conditional promises, with the condition clearly given in vs 1:

> *IF* you will listen carefully to the voice of the Lord your God, watching to do all that He Commands that I command you this day, then the Lord will set you on high above all the nations of the earth.

Then come the promises—with this wonderful preamble, Deuteronomy 28:2:

> These blessings will come upon you and overtake
> you, if you will take notice of the Lord your God.

I really do not know what would overtake what, in an
Old Testament situation—perhaps a chariot might overtake an
ox-cart, but this makes wonderful sense to us today. Can you
imagine the promises you've underlined in your Bible
scooting down the freeway and dodging their way past you to
get to your destination before you do?

Every single one of these promises is so very clearly
for here and now. They are all so wonderfully practical. These
are not esoteric pie-in-the-sky; these are practical promises for
our every-day here-and-now.

So as you work down this wonderful list of promises,
remember that Jesus fulfilled all of those terms and conditions
on your behalf. Now very clearly, if you want to make the
most of these promises then it makes sense to live cognisant
and obedient to those conditions. The key is that our failure,
especially our failure in times past, is not a disqualification to
receiving that promise now.

But while looking through all the precious promises
listed in Deuteronomy 28 we need to watch out for some
verses near the end of the chapter, verses 45-48:

> All these curses will come on you. They will pursue
> you and overtake you until you are
> destroyed, because you did not obey the Lord your
> God and observe the commands and decrees He gave
> you. They will be a sign and a wonder to you and
> your descendants forever, because you did not
> serve the Lord *your God joyfully and gladly in the
> time of prosperity.*

I haven't included this to bring condemnation. Jesus
bore the penalty for our sin, so for those of us living out of that

forgiven relationship with Him, then our failure here in this regard no longer has these consequences as they are covered by His Blood. But this is a powerfully simple reminder of the importance of serving the Lord joyfully and thankfully, especially in times of prosperity. This is so important as an attitude towards the Lord to bring Him Joy, to help us align ourselves to make it easy for Him to bless us and to keep the door firmly shut on the one whom so loves to steal, kill and destroy.

I have spelled out each of the promises and how we could see and apply them for ourselves today, in my book *Mercy—God's Covenant assistance*, Chapter 17:

Vs 3, You will be blessed in the city and blessed in the country. (NIV)

At home or at work—blessing everywhere. (And in between!)

Blessed at home, and blessed on holiday.

Vs 4, The fruit of your womb will be blessed, and the crops of your land and the young of your livestock— the calves of your herds and the lambs of your flocks. (NIV)

No barrenness anywhere, no miscarriage—your marriage, your pets, your garden, your business, your ideas, your inventions, your plans, your dreams....blessed.

Vs 5, Your basket and your kneading trough will be blessed. (NIV)

Your fridge and your freezer—will be full—and they will last a looooong time.

In your bread-bin and store-cupboards there will always be more than enough.

Vs 6, You will be blessed when you come in and blessed when you go out. (NIV)

Now what do you go out and come in—in? Your car of course! (Are you driving your dream car?) And your doorway and drive will be blessed. You don't need to fear coming in to find the place ransacked.

Vs 7, The LORD will grant that the enemies who rise up against you will be defeated before you. They will come at you from one direction but flee from you in seven. (NIV)

I wonder what you fear most... no don't get to thinking, or like Job you will be inviting those very things to descend on you. The intent here is exactly the opposite. Whatever that may be—those enemies that come against you one way, **flee before you seven ways**, be it redundancy—divorce—bankruptcy—humiliation—loneliness...

Oh, how much we need this next one:

Deuteronomy 28:8:
The LORD will send a blessing on your barns and on everything you put your hand to. The LORD your God will bless you in the land he is giving you. (NIV)

Your bank balance and your credit rating—BLESSED!
But you do need to be putting your hand to something... and you will be blessed right where you are.

Vs 9, The LORD will establish you as His holy people, as he promised you on oath, if you keep the commands of the LORD your God and walk in His ways. (NIV)

Vs 10, Then all the peoples on earth will see that you are called by the name of the LORD, and they will fear you. (NIV)

And here is a taste of the reason—so that everyone around you sees that the Lord is the one who is blessing you and gets envious and drawn to Him—by looking at the blessings pouring into your lap.

> Vs 11, The LORD will grant you abundant prosperity—in the fruit of your womb, the young of your livestock and the crops of your ground—in the land he swore to your forefathers to give you. (NIV)

Abundant Prosperity—what more can anyone ask for? And surely this encompasses far more than just direct material things, though clearly they are important. But this also has to do with dreams and longings, with favour and influence, with relationships and family, with the outcome of your efforts, especially in areas way outside of your control.

> Vs 12, The LORD will open the heavens, the storehouse of his bounty, to send rain on your land in season and to bless all the work of your hands. You will lend to many nations but will borrow from none. (NIV)

The borrower is always subject to the lender. So if you are going to be free, then you have to be the lender; and this draws those to you to share and receive of the blessings He is pouring into your life and family. This has to be more than enough to liberally bless others—especially God's people—and His ministries.

> Vs 13, The LORD will make you the head, not the tail. If you pay attention to the commands of the LORD your God that I give you this day and carefully follow them, you will always be at the top, never at the bottom. (NIV)

Now for most of us, we can look at those promises and laugh much like Sarah did in the back of the tent. But this is our God's love and intent for each and every one of us.

Covenant Partnership

These are our Heavenly Dad's, our Covenant Partner's promises—His longing, His heart and desire for each one of us. Now that does not mean these simply fall into our lap, though some of them may. No—rather these are promises to bring out and take to the court of Heaven as and when needed. So when the bleeding starts threatening an impending miscarriage, you take verse 4 with your bread and your cup and remind your Covenant Partner of His Covenant Promise to you.

Chapter 7   Cutting Covenant

Formulating and entering into a covenant relationship with someone requires the shedding of blood, so is called 'cutting covenant'. Typically this requires cutting the two parties and collecting their blood and mixing it. This is why such a covenant is often called a blood covenant.

In every culture, such a covenant is a weighty sacrificial business. Cutting covenant always requires sacrifice. Our western marriage covenant is sealed by the exchange of rings that are not insignificant in their cost and value to each party. Sacrifice, in one form or another, is essential to covenant. Remember this is a legal transaction with the full force of law behind it.

Cutting a blood covenant is a serious business with long-lasting ramifications. When Abimelech and Phicol, his chief captain, saw the blessing of the Lord on Abraham, they wanted to cut covenant with him, Genesis 21:22. Abraham called the place where they did this, Beersheba, which means 'well of covenant', Genesis 21:31. Abraham then went on to plant a tamarisk tree there, a very slow-growing evergreen tree, Genesis 21:33, to mark the spot. Such a tree takes hundreds of years to grow to its full size, so is planted for later generations. It is an evergreen tree. Such a covenant does not change with the seasons.

The details of cutting covenant have varied from culture to culture. Even in biblical times and in biblical cultures are a number of different descriptions. In every occasion it is a weighty, costly and sacrificial event reflecting the weightiness of what is being entered into and the costly commitment involved. We devalue the huge cost paid by Jesus, if we disrespect this priceless covenant that He sealed between humankind and Father God, at the cost of His own blood and suffering, *by not drawing on it.*

One aspect of Jesus' death was as the Covenant sacrificial offering, for this wonderful covenant between God and man. It required a man and a perfect man who had never sinned, to freely offer Himself, to fulfil this sacrificial offering. As the Son of Man, His Blood was the blood of a man, and as the Son of God, His Blood was equally the blood of God. His Life, His Body, His Blood and His Death represents and fulfils the two parties in Himself.

As I outlined in Chapter 2, Genesis 15 gives us a wonderful description of God cutting covenant with Abram. Apparently in this era the custom was to lay out the sacrificial carcasses and the two parties were to walk together between them.

1 Samuel 18 we have a description of Saul's son Jonathan cutting covenant with David. Here, Jonathan the Prince, the eldest son of King Saul, the first in line to the throne, exchanges his princely robe, his sword, his bow and his belt, with David.

As the writer to the Hebrews mentions in Chapter 6: 16:

When two people cut covenant they do so before someone of higher authority, to hold them accountable. Often this will be with a priest invoking the cursing of their particular god or gods, should they break their covenant promises to each other.

L & B Translation

In the previous chapter I quoted the blessings that were to result from the Mosaic Covenant as set down by Moses in Deuteronomy Chapter 28. The second half of this chapter, verses 16 to verse 68, is a mirror, declaring the curses that would come upon them if they failed to observe the commandments and statutes that they agreed upon in the terms of the covenant. These were the blessings and curses they agreed to on entering their promised land.

Moses formalised this very clearly for them, for when they would cross over the Jordan. They were to make an altar to the Lord in a valley and write out there the words of the law, verse 8. Then six of the tribes were to stand on Mount Gerazim and declare the blessings, and six were to stand opposite Mount Gerazim, on Mount Ebal and declare the curses. Deuteronomy 27:15-26 are the actions that would initiate the curses.

Thank God our New Covenant is not like that! Now please don't get me wrong, if you want the blessings then it pays to look at those conditions, in order to end up with them. But the moment we look at the spirit behind the conditions we rapidly realize our difficulty with fulfilling them. But Jesus was made a curse for us through being nailed to a tree, Deuteronomy 21:23, so He bore every curse for us.

Jesus bore every curse that we bring upon ourselves, and every curse that others may try and put on us. He bore every curse that should have been ours, in our place, Isaiah 53:11, He shall bear their iniquities. Similarly sin is not an issue in our New Covenant. Under the Old Covenant, the sacrifices covered over sin and hence needed to be regularly repeated. But as the writer to the Hebrews so succinctly put it:

> What the Old Covenant could never do, the New Covenant achieved at a stroke. We who have received Jesus as our Lord and Saviour are all declared perfect before God through that one single sacrifice that Jesus, the Anointed Messiah, went through on the cross.　　Hebrews 10:10
> *L & B Translation*

Chapter 8   Covenant Relationship

This Covenant relationship is hugely more than highlighting promises. This is about living out a Covenantal *relationship* with All-Mighty God! This is a legally binding relationship with the full weight of law behind it.

So what does this look like?

Just how does this work?

We have some excellent examples in the Bible for us, Abraham, Moses and David are three very different people for us to follow, whose lives I explore in the following chapters.

Just as in a marriage covenant, each partner adds their dreams and longing to the other in mutual fulfilment. Each of these men found the fulfilment of their deepest dreams and longings outworked through their Covenant Relationship with the All-Mighty-One.

But our God, our Heavenly Dad, always thinks multi-generationally as He lives outside of time. The three examples whose lives I have explored in the following chapters were all blessed in a measure, but the Lord had a significantly greater depth of fulfilment planned for their succeeding generations. His promises to them were so much bigger, deeper and wider than they appreciated, or experienced in their own lives.

The writer to the Hebrews captures something of this in celebrating those who never see in their lifetime, the fulfilment of what is promised to them:

These, and many others, died never seeing the fulfilment of their specific promise that they lived in faith for. They caught glimpses of it, but lived and referred to themselves as foreigners and desert nomads on the earth. They demonstrated they were searching for a very different city. If what they had left behind had any value to them, they had plenty of time to go back to it. We can see they were looking for something a whole lot better—they were looking for Heaven here, and because of this, Father God Himself is delighted to be known as their God, for He has prepared just the very place (the Heavenly New Jerusalem) for them.

Hebrews 11:13-16   *L and B Translation*

These people are celebrated for their faith even though they never personally received what they had been promised; they are celebrated just as much as those who did receive. We will never know the depths of their relationship, their intimacy, with the One who Jesus asked us to call our Heavenly Dad. In Old Covenant times He was known as YHWH which was so Holy, so awesome, so as-it-were untouchable, as to never be spoken aloud. So to be more in keeping with their framework I will revert here onwards to more standard biblical language—this will also flow more readily with the quoted verses. What is very clear from the examples I have taken is their intimacy with Him; how they each knew His character and His ways, oftentimes better than many New Covenant believers. And this could also be said of many other Old Covenant characters.

The three examples I explore next, each had very different dreams and longings. Akin to their individual destinies, they each found and received a measure of fulfilment. Abraham had his 'child-of-promise', his Isaac, and through his succeeding generations raised a family from which the ultimate Redeemer would come and thereby all the nations of the earth be blessed. The land of Canaan was promised to his descendants, although Abraham lived there almost as an outcast!

Moses knew he wanted to see his people, his nation, set free from slavery in Egypt, but it took 80 years before he had matured to the point where God could use him. Clearly Moses was aware of his destiny long before. God's dream was not just to see the people freed from their slavery, but equipped to live in freedom before they entered their 'promised land'. Evidently it took 40 years of traipsing around the wilderness to get that slavery mentality out of them.

We will never know what David's dreams and longings were for his life as a shepherd boy minding his father's sheep on the hillside, as he learned to lean on and worship the Lord. I suspect they were very similar to Abraham's, especially as he would have been taught Abraham's story, over and over again. As king, he completed Joshua's mandate to conquer and occupy the whole of the land the Lord originally assigned to the people of Israel. But he wasn't content to stop there! Having built his own palace, he dreamed of building a palace for the Lord and the Ark of the Covenant. But oh how I love the Lord's response, that He would build David's house—that He would build David's family line with one of his descendants *forever* on the throne. How wonderfully this expresses the heart of reciprocity that is a key facet of a Covenant Relationship.

I wonder what your dream and destiny looks like? It took me many years to even catch a glimpse of mine. David captured his in a simple statement, and when you have discovered yours, you will probably equally have it condensed into a single simple statement. David may have taken a whole Psalm to express it in its fullness, but he wrote,

Here's the one thing I crave from God, the one thing I seek above all else: I want the privilege of living with him every moment in his house, finding the sweet loveliness of his face, filled with awe, delighting in his glory and grace. I want to live my life so close to him that he takes pleasure in my every prayer.

Psalm 27:4 The Passion Translation®

Looking at each of these lives, we see Abraham, Moses and David growing in their relationship and trust with the Lord over many years. Even after the Lord cut covenant with him, Abram still has a lot of learning to do, before the Lord fulfils that promise to him of a son. After the cutting of that covenant, when the Lord reminds Abraham that he is going to have that son, Abraham still falls about laughing at the absurdity of it, Genesis 17:17.

So even when a covenant relationship has been established, it still takes time to grow. David is described as only a youth at the time of his anointing as king by Samuel in 1 Samuel 16:10-13, i.e. probably no older than fifteen. But he wasn't formally anointed and recognised by the tribe of Judah until he was thirty, and it was another seven years and six months before he was anointed king over all Israel and Judah, 2 Samuel 5:4-5.

And so it is with us, that when we are anointed by Holy Spirit and brought into this covenant relationship with our Heavenly Dad, we have to grow in that relationship.

One key thing that emerges from all three of these examples is their longing to know the Lord better, more intimately, to know His Heart, His Ways and His Presence. Abraham got to know Him well enough to instantly recognise Him when He turns up at his tent as described for us in Genesis 18. One of Moses' key prayers is for the Lord to show him His Glory, Exodus 33:18. This is Moses' heart.

Moses was known as one who spoke with Him face-to-face, Deuteronomy 34:10. He had the most incredible revelation of what heaven looked like that he had to reproduce here on the earth, both in the design of the tabernacle, and also in the nature of how to live with Heaven's government in their Promised Land. And it was said of Moses that he knew His Ways whereas the children of Israel only saw His Acts, Psalm 103:7. In other words, the people never saw through those acts into the Lord's Heart, and ways.

Similarly, David's heart is revealed to us over and over in the Psalms, reinforcing the validity of Samuel's word to Saul about the man who Jehovah was appointing to replace him as king, that Jehovah sought him a man after his own heart, 1 Samuel 13:14. It is said that David set the Ark of the Covenant on a table in the tent of worship that he set up next to his palace. He set it on a table so he could go and lie under it to be as close as he could get to 'The Presence', looking at the wings of the cherubim spreading out beyond the lid, and this was what he was alluding to in referring to being under the shadow of His Wings—Psalm 17:8 & Psalm 36:7.

With the tenderness of such an intimate and binding relationship, comes a weighty responsibility. From a distance, all that many see is the Lord's judgment. The ten commandments are clearly black and white. It is so easy to point to sin with its inevitable consequences of judgment. It requires an intimacy with Him to see the other side of His Character and Nature that He so longs for an excuse to bring Mercy instead. Like a just judge in a courtroom when the case is clearly done and dusted, that judgment is deserved and the verdict is unequivocal. However much he may want to, he cannot give a merciful verdict unless an appropriate case can be made, or he would be unjust.

When we see sin, evil and injustice, does our heart cry out for justice? We have a mighty and weighty responsibility to see it for precisely what it is. We have a responsibility to feel the weight of the evil and injustice, its hurt and pain, and to carry this into the Lord's Presence. It is from His internally transforming Love, that we go on to make the case and plead for mercy. From a distance, the evil, and the hurt, the pain and loss that resulted from that evil, does not fully register in us. To those with hearts of love we can scarcely comprehend the hearts of those who plot evil and control, murder and thievery, mockery of our Saviour Jesus and the huge price that He paid to forgive us and adopt us into His family. But when we are up close and personal, when it directly affects us and those who we love, then it causes us to shout for justice. But we are called to go on from there and into that intimate place with Him, so that our heart is transformed to become like His, such that we long to bring Mercy in place of judgment. That's a very tough assignment. That requires a deep level of loving our enemies, forgiving and loving them while hating their sin. Mercy triumphs over justice James 2:13.

This is the story of Stephen in Acts 6-7. He saw the evil of the accusers raised against him:

> Ye stiffnecked and uncircumcised in heart and ears, ye do always resist the Holy Ghost: as your father did, so do ye. Which of the prophets have not your fathers persecuted? And they have slain them which showed before of the coming of the Just One; of whom ye have been now the betrayers and murderers: who have received the law by the disposition of angels, and have not kept it.

> Acts 7:51-53

But Stephen's response at the end was:

> He kneeled down, and cried with a loud voice, Lord, lay not this sin to their charge. And when he had said this, he fell asleep.

> Acts 7:60

The psalmist touches on this in Psalm 73. For the first 16 verses he is bewildered, frustrated and appalled by the evil of those around him with no sign of justice. But as he says in verse 17, when he went into the sanctuary and drew close to the Lord, he began to see the bigger picture, and describes it as like waking from a dream. His soul was grieved and his heart pricked as he realized just how brutish and ignorant he had become while away from the presence of the Lord. [Verses 20-22.]

The Lord needs us to construct a case for Mercy to be shown, and shown to the very people whose evil has impacted us. If we had glimpsed the horrors of hell and the nature of eternal judgment then maybe like the psalmist we would find this easier to do. I'm not suggesting this is easy, or comes naturally. It doesn't! It only comes from imbibing our Daddy's sweet Nature and drinking of His sweet Spirit from spending time in His Presence. In His Presence, we appreciate something of how precious and sweet His transformation is to our hearts, and how much we value and need that which has been so freely given to us, which we never deserved for a moment.

Abraham, Moses and David were put in this situation a number of times, especially Moses.

Chapter 9   Abraham as our Example

Abram, later renamed Abraham comes first so I'll start with looking at the life of Abraham.

Abram's father had moved the family from Ur to Harran. (Genesis 11:31) They were intending to move to Canaan but stopped and settled in Harran. In Genesis 12 the Lord says to Abram "Go from your country, your people and your father's household to the land I will show you."

Along with this came a wonderful promise of blessing, blessing and more blessing (see Genesis 12:2-3.) Strictly this is a conditional promise on him leaving Harran for someplace, who knows where... and Abram took Lot and Lot's family with him, so he didn't exactly fulfil the precise details the Lord had given him.

East of Bethel in Genesis 12:8 and later in Mamre, in Genesis 13:18, Abram erected altars to the Lord where the Lord appeared to him on his journey. So he clearly loved the Lord and had a very special relationship with Him, but so far there is no mention of a covenant. It is not until chapter 15 that we see the Lord cutting covenant with Abram, precisely because Abram is struggling to believe the Lord's promises. He even goes as far to ask the Lord in verse 8, "How can I know that I will gain possession of it?" It is in response to this that the Lord goes on to cutting covenant with Abram in Genesis 15:9-21.

In verse 17 the Lord passed between the pieces that Abram had spread out. Normally both parties would walk together between the pieces, signifying their mutual agreement. But here Abram was in a deep sleep, and it is only the Lord who is walking between the pieces, so the Lord is making it clear to Abram that this is an unconditional covenant

—it is dependent upon the Lord only. In this context it was not dependent upon anything that Abram did, or said, or thought.

Turning over the page to the next chapter—Genesis 16, both Abram and Sarai are still struggling with the reality of this. Sarai comes up with a crazy plan of engineering this in man's way. She tells Abram to go and have intercourse with her slave Hagar and have a child through her—to which Abram agreed. Needless to say this brought trouble and problems from the moment Hagar knew she was pregnant!

Chapter 17 begins with another stage in this process. Once more the Lord appears to Abram to confirm that covenant promise made in chapter 15. At this point Abram fell about laughing—verse 17. The Lord does spell out in verse 9 the condition of circumcision for this next promise. In Abraham's next encounter in Chapter 18, Sarah was listening at the entrance to the tent and she laughed too at the absurdity of the Lord's promise to her—verse 12, but she only laughed 'to herself' i.e. inwardly—but sufficient for the Lord to notice as given in verse 13. So the Lord repeats His promise to her, just to emphasise the point. And Oh I so love the next two verses! "Sarah was afraid, so she lied and said, 'I did not laugh.' But the Lord said, 'Yes you did laugh.'"

Here is no shame or condemnation for her unbelief, but rather the gentle loving embrace of the truth. This is the God and Heavenly Dad we have!

Let us never forget that His Promises to us are equally, absurdly, above and beyond our wildest dreams, in precisely those areas closest to our hearts.

Abraham clearly walked in a close relationship with the Lord, as we are called to do. In chapter 18, when the Lord appeared with two others, Abraham instantly recognised Him, bowed low before Him (in worship) and invited Him in for a meal. He ran off to find Sarah to make all the preparations, verses 1-7. Remember that angels always insist that they are not to be worshipped, but God alone.

And in spite of such an intimate relationship, and his unconditional covenant with the Lord, Abraham and Sarah are still struggling to believe the Lord's promise to them. Oh there's hope for us yet!

If the Lord came knocking on your door, would you recognise Him, or like the disciples on the Emmaus road would you have no idea? And there are times when He does indeed come knocking, when it is all too easy to miss Him, and it is up to us to open the door to Him—Revelation 3:20.

And as Genesis chapter 18 progresses, another key aspect of this relationship unfolds. As his guests get up to leave, Abraham accompanies them on their way. At which point the Lord opens up with "Shall I hide from Abraham what I am about to do?" Such is this covenant relationship with Abraham that he is in the loop with what the Lord is planning on doing. This is the weighty responsibility of those with a covenant partnership with the Lord. Here he reasons with the Lord, exactly as described by Isaiah 1:18:

Come let us reason together, saith the Lord: though your sins be as scarlet, they shall be white as snow. (KJV)

He is looking for those who will give Him the legal evidence to be merciful. He was looking to find a legal reason why *not* to destroy Sodom and Gomorrah, which Abraham tried hard to offer.

If we look at the life of Moses leading the people of Israel through the wilderness he repeatedly had to do precisely this and plead appropriate reasons why the Lord should not simply wipe out the whole nation.

Will you be pleading Mercy or Judgment? From a look at the number of judgment prophetic words it certainly appears that many prophets today are giving the wrong message. Do you and I have ingrained in our psyche that Mercy *triumphs* over Justice? Do we share the Lord's Heart to desperately search out reasons for Him to be Merciful, when there is every reason for His Judgment? Please, please remember our own need for His Mercy, that 'there but for the Grace of God go you and I.' We too deserve His Judgment just as much as anyone. Mercy, by definition, is never deserved. Our covenant responsibility is huge, so I have given this a whole chapter, in Chapter 19.

The next key point I want to raise in Abraham's story is Genesis chapter 22. It is not clear just how old Isaac would have been, or how long since the Lord cut covenant with Abraham, promising that his whole family line would be blessed through Isaac. Assuming the story is told chronologically, Chapter 23 with the account of Sarah's death at one hundred and twenty seven, Isaac must have been less than thirty seven years old. Many theologians believe Isaac to have been in his early thirties and if he was a type and forerunner of Jesus, he may well have been thirty three years old, the same age as Jesus at His Crucifixion. Genesis 22, verse 2 the Lord asks Abraham to offer Isaac as a burnt offering. Now this makes no sense in the absence of any comprehension of covenant. But a covenant is a bilateral agreement. It is reciprocal—any help I need, then I ask my covenant partner to provide and similarly they can ask me—on the basis of our covenant agreement. So here the Lord is asking Abraham for a redeeming sacrifice. In the context of the child-sacrificing worship of Molech, by the people around him, this is not quite as unreasonable as may appear to us now, and as Christians, we are acutely aware of our need for a Redeemer, as provided for us by Jesus!

When Israel (Jacob) comes to bless Joseph's sons, he begins his blessing with a wonderful description of the God to whom he is asking to give this blessing. It is very interesting how he describes this God who he has come to know and trust, see Genesis 48:15-16:

> God, before whom my fathers Abraham and Isaac did walk, the God which fed me all my life long unto this day, the angel which redeemed me from all evil, bless the lads. (KJV)

This is the God who Jacob has come to know. This is the God who he is asking to bless the lads—the One who has fed him (provided for him) all his life and the One who is His Redeemer. Could you describe your God so succinctly?

So the patriarchs clearly knew they needed a Redeemer —just as we do. Israel [Jacob] referred to him as an angel, but no angel can redeem—this is simply language for Jesus—the man—our Redeemer. Israel knew and had a relationship with his Redeemer. We don't know the timeframe of the story of Job, but even he declared in Job 19:25 "I know that my Redeemer liveth, and he will stand at the latter day upon the earth," (KJV).

Back to Genesis Chapter 22 and Abraham offering his son as a burnt offering; he is doing something far more than responding to a test of faith. He is here effectively saying to his covenant partner, I am prepared to offer my son as a burnt offering, inadequate though that will be. So are you prepared to offer your perfect son to be my Redeemer?

Here Abraham is obligating Father God. His Dad, his Covenant Partner, to offer His Son to be our Redeemer.

So when Isaac asks "where is the lamb?" in verse 7, Abraham's answer in verse 8 that "God will provide", is precisely the nature of the whole encounter. Was Abraham expecting Isaac, the very one promised to him as the one through whom all the promises regarding his inheritance would be fulfilled, would be brought back to life after the sacrifice? This is certainly inferred by Abraham all but going through with slaughtering Isaac as the sacrifice, but from his statement to Isaac at the foot of the mountain, he was clearly expecting his God to provide.

This is the role of a covenant partner, of mutual agreement. When one is in need, they ask the other to provide. When the Lord needed a legal advocate to refrain from bringing just judgment on Sodom and Gomorrah (Genesis 18), he came to Abraham. When Abraham recognised his need of a redeemer who only Father God could provide, he stepped in and obligated Father God, his Covenant Partner, to provide.

As His Covenant Partner you walk in His Courts, as much as you walk this earth. You are called into His Council, and He too has an ear for the needs of the situations you walk in, that you bring to Him. Indeed this is your responsibility. Remember the Lord's words to Abraham that He says to us today, "Is anything too hard for the Lord? Genesis 18:14.

I am writing this in the middle of the coronavirus crisis—so what request is appropriate to bring to Him 'for whom nothing is impossible'? This is indeed the role of a Covenant Partner with the Most High. My thought would be that the whole pandemic dies as rapidly as it has arisen, across the globe. The devil's over-riding ambition is to upset and delay the Lord's timing and thereby thwart the Lord's plans and purposes. This ambition needs to be countered. Wisdom and insight is needed, especially to those developing vaccines with innovative ways of proving them and producing them in sufficient quantity. And wisdom and insight too, over the use of existing drugs that may make the requirement for vaccines completely unnecessary.

But alongside that, we see the Lord using this for His own purposes, to bring a reset and real Passover, with the second wave coinciding precisely with Rosh Hashanah and Yom Kippur. Not since that first Passover in Egypt has Passover been not just practised, but widely observed. In Exodus 12:17 the Lord declared that this Passover celebration was to be observed annually as an ordinance for ever, and Jewish families have indeed continued to celebrate these festivals very much as Moses outlined there in Exodus. But never before have so many nations effectively locked down their whole populations so closely observing Rosh Hashanah and Yom Kippur.

But back to Abraham's story. He desperately wanted a son and heir who carried his DNA, who was genuinely bone of his bone, flesh of his flesh. But this was the Lord's dream and longing too! He wanted a man who would raise his children to know Him, so each succeeding generation would grow in revelation, understanding and love in their relationship with Him, so that ultimately through this line He could bring His Son. This was the father He was looking for and this makes sense of the other dream in Abraham's heart that the writer to the Hebrews captured so clearly for us, in Hebrews 11:8-10. As Abraham went out from the place where his father had settled, he was looking, longing and searching for a city whose foundation, whose 'raison d'être' was in their Covenant relationship with Father God, only here would be 'home' for him, surrounded by others pursuing and living in this precious relationship with God.

> It was by faith in the promise the Lord gave him that Abraham left Ur of the Chaldees. The promise was that he needed to leave home if he was to receive an inheritance. He left with no clue as to where he was going. By faith, he lived in tents with his son Isaac

and grandson Jacob, as a traveller in a foreign land, when all the time he was actually living in the land which was promised to him. [But he didn't realise this was going to be his inheritance, and at one point he ended up wandering through and out the other side of it.] Isaac and Jacob were also heirs of the promise made to Abraham. He was looking for a city, for a land, founded on a relationship with the God who had entered into covenant relationship with Him.   Hebrews 11:8-10   *L & B Translation*

Are you struggling to find your tribe? Are you, like Abraham, struggling to find a people who share your hunger for a real relationship with The Almighty One, or struggling to find those who like to give expression to that in the same way as you?

What emerges from looking at each of these three examples I explore in this book is that the Lord always thinks multi-generationally.

What 'qualified' Abraham to have this intimacy with the Lord? This is almost certainly not what you would have anticipated as the qualification:

Genesis 18:17-19   And the Lord said, Shall I hide from Abraham that thing which I do; seeing that Abraham shall surely become a great and mighty nation, and all the nations of the earth shall be blessed in him? For I know him, that he will command his children and his household after them, and they shall keep the way of the Lord, to do justice and judgment; that the Lord may bring upon Abraham that which He hath spoken of him. (KJV)

Chapter 10 Moses the Covenant Broker

Moses was evidently brought up well aware of his family background, their oppression, their slavery and injustice. Exodus doesn't tell us just how old he was when he killed the Egyptian who was mistreating a Hebrew as given in Exodus 2:11. His destiny was deeply ingrained into him by this point, though far from clear just how he was going to work this out. For many years I had absolutely no idea what my destiny was, or what I would like to do, though I gleaned a fair idea somewhat earlier than Moses who didn't get his burning bush God-mandated call to return to Egypt until he was 80, Exodus 7:7.

Like so many of us, when we do get an inkling of what that destiny call requires of us, Moses pulled out every conceivable reason why he was not the man for the job till the Lord became quite angry with him, Exodus 4:14! Finally, the Lord agreed that Aaron, his younger brother, could speak for him. One advantage of being way out of our depth, is that we rely and trust Him rather than relying on our own abilities.

As we look at Moses' ministry we see time and again his true heart revealed. Again and again he lays his life on the line on behalf of the people and even his own brother and sister at one point. Although he never led the people into their Promised Land himself, he knew he had raised up an assistant who would, and that his dream and longing would be fulfilled by the next generation. He secured the Lord's promise that He would go with them—always. I guess there were many times when he realised just how impossible his dream was. It was one thing to get the people out of Egypt, but it was quite another to get Egypt out of them!

Moses' initial request to Pharaoh is quite revealing of his heart in declaring that Pharaoh was to let the people go and worship the God of Israel in the wilderness (Exodus 5:1). Clearly his heart is that all the people get to know and worship the God who he had encountered. No mention was made at that point that this was to be permanent!

There are times, such as when we have slipped into sin, or had things stolen from us, especially spiritual things, or cutting generational ties, when we have to take a case before the Court of Heaven, presenting our case before the just Judge. But sometimes we have to come before our Covenant Partner and plead the case of others on their behalf. This has nothing to do with what they deserve, but it has everything to do with ·our relationship with Him. This is epitomised by Moses time and again having to plead on behalf of the people.

To add to Moses' issues, he is repeatedly facing the people of Israel in the wilderness viciously complaining at the Lord, *and him*, and even his own family complaining about him in Numbers 12. The following excerpts from Exodus and Numbers illustrate some of these moments and I have italicised Moses' words as he pleads the people's case in intercession, as a Covenant Partner with the Lord. These are all from the (KJV). This is far from exhaustive—if this piques your interest then there is much there for more in-depth study.

See Exodus 17:2 where the people are thirsting for water:

Wherefore the people strove with Moses, and said, "Give us water that we may drink." And Moses said unto them, "Why strive ye with me? Wherefore do ye tempt Jehovah?" [3] And the people thirsted there for water; and the people murmured against Moses, and said, "Wherefore hast thou brought us up out of Egypt, to kill us and our children and our cattle with thirst?" [4] And Moses cried unto Jehovah, saying, "What shall I do unto this people? they are almost ready to stone me." ⁵ And Jehovah said unto Moses, "Pass on before the people, and take with thee of the elders of Israel; and thy rod, wherewith thou smotest the river, take in thy hand, and go. ⁶ Behold, I will stand before thee there upon the rock in Horeb; and thou shalt smite the rock, and there shall come water out of it, that the people may drink." And Moses did so in the sight of the elders of Israel. ⁷ And he called the name of the place Massah, and Meribah, because of the striving of the children of Israel, and because they tempted Jehovah, saying, "Is Jehovah among us, or not?"

In Exodus 32:9-14 the people are worshipping the golden calf, while Moses is up on the mountain:

And Jehovah said unto Moses, "I have seen this people, and, behold, it is a stiffnecked people: ¹⁰ now therefore let Me alone, that My Wrath may wax hot against them, and that I may consume them: and I will make of thee a great nation." ¹¹ And Moses besought Jehovah his God, and said, *"Jehovah, why doth Thy Wrath wax hot against Thy People, that Thou hast brought forth out of the land of Egypt with great power and with a mighty hand? ¹² Wherefore should the Egyptians speak, saying, For evil did He bring them forth, to slay them in the mountains, and to consume them from the face of the earth? Turn from Thy Fierce Wrath, and repent of this evil against Thy People. ¹³ Remember Abraham, Isaac, and Israel, Thy Servants, to whom Thou swarest by Thine own self, and saidst unto them, I will multiply your seed as the stars of heaven, and all this land that I have spoken of will I give unto your seed, and they shall inherit it for ever."* ¹⁴ And Jehovah

repented of the evil which He said He would do unto
His people.   (Italics mine.)

So here Moses starts off by highlighting that if the Lord did what He had said, then His Reputation would be in tatters. He then moves on to the promises the Lord had given to the Patriarchs highlighting the Lord's Faithfulness to His Word (Psalm 138:2 "He will honor His Word over and above even His very Name!")

The story continues:

Exodus 32:15-20:

And Moses turned, and went down from the mount, with the two tables of the testimony in his hand; tables that were written on both their sides; on the one side and on the other were they written. [16] And the tables were the work of God, and the writing was the writing of God, graven upon the tables. [17] And when Joshua heard the noise of the people as they shouted, he said unto Moses, There is a noise of war in the camp. [18] And he said, "It is not the voice of them that shout for mastery, neither is it the voice of them that cry for being overcome; but the noise of them that sing do I hear." [19] And it came to pass, as soon as he came nigh unto the camp, that he saw the calf and the dancing: and Moses' anger waxed hot, and he cast the tables out of his hands, and break them beneath the mount.

Exodus 32:30-35:

And it came to pass on the morrow, that Moses said unto the people, "Ye have sinned a great sin: and now I will go up unto Jehovah; peradventure I shall make atonement for your sin." [31] And Moses returned unto Jehovah, and said, "*Oh, this people*

have sinned a great sin, and have made them gods of
gold. ³² Yet now, if Thou wilt forgive their sin—; and
if not, blot me, I pray Thee, out of Thy Book which
Thou hast written." ³³ And Jehovah said unto Moses,
"Whosoever hath sinned against Me, him will I blot
out of My Book. ³⁴ And now go, lead the people
unto the place of which I have spoken unto thee:
behold, Mine angel shall go before thee; nevertheless
in the day when I visit, I will visit their sin upon
them." ³⁵ And Jehovah smote the people, because
they made the calf, which Aaron made.

Here Moses acknowledges the people's sin to the Lord
and takes it upon himself. I'm not sure I would so readily
volunteer to be blotted out of the Lord's Book of Life for
someone else. So in spite of Moses pleading their case, He
could only take it so far. Many of those who had played their
part in the setting up and worship of the golden calf clearly
didn't survive. But Moses catches something that the Lord let
slip in Exodus 33:2 & 3, that he wasn't prepared to run with—
that the Lord would not go with them, but only an angel.
Exodus 33:11-23:

> And Jehovah spake unto Moses face to face, as a
> man speaketh unto his friend. And he turned again
> into the camp: but his minister Joshua, the son of
> Nun, a young man, departed not out of the Tent.
>
> ¹² And Moses said unto Jehovah, "See, Thou sayest
> unto me, "Bring up this people: and Thou hast not let
> me know whom Thou wilt send with me. Yet Thou
> hast said, I know thee by name, and Thou hast also
> found favor in My Sight. ¹³ Now therefore, I pray
> Thee, if I have found favor in Thy Sight, show me
> now Thy Ways, that I may know Thee, to the end
> that I may find favor in Thy Sight: and consider that

this nation is Thy People." ¹⁴ And He said, "My Presence shall go with thee, and I will give thee rest." ¹⁵ And he said unto Him, "*If Thy Presence go not with me, carry us not up hence. ¹⁶ For wherein now shall it be known that I have found favor in Thy Sight, I and Thy People? is it not in that Thou goest with us, so that we are separated, I and Thy People, from all the people that are upon the face of the earth?*"

¹⁷ And Jehovah said unto Moses, "I will do this thing also that thou hast spoken; for thou hast found favor in My Sight, and I know thee by name." ¹⁸ And he said, "Show me, I pray thee, Thy Glory." ¹⁹ And He said, "I will make all My Goodness pass before thee, and will proclaim the Name of Jehovah before thee; and I will be gracious to whom I will be gracious, and will show mercy on whom I will show mercy." ²⁰ And He said, "Thou canst not see My Face; for man shall not see Me and live." ²¹ And Jehovah said, "Behold, there is a place by Me, and thou shalt stand upon the rock: ²² and it shall come to pass, while My Glory passeth by, that I will put thee in a cleft of the rock, and will cover thee with My hand until I have passed by: ²³ and I will take away My Hand, and thou shalt see My Back; but My Face shall not be seen."

The Lord did exactly that, as described in the following chapter:
Exodus 34:5-10:

And Jehovah descended in the cloud, and stood with him there, and proclaimed the Name of Jehovah. ⁶ And Jehovah passed by before him, and proclaimed, Jehovah, Jehovah, a God Merciful and

Gracious, slow to anger, and abundant in Lovingkindness and Truth; [7] keeping Lovingkindness for thousands, forgiving iniquity and transgression and sin; and that will by no means clear the guilty, visiting the iniquity of the fathers upon the children, and upon the children's children, upon the third and upon the fourth generation. [8] And Moses made haste, and bowed his head toward the earth, and worshipped. [9] And he said, "If now I have found favor in Thy Sight, O Lord, let the Lord, I pray Thee, go in the midst of us; for it is a stiffnecked people; and pardon our iniquity and our sin, and take us for Thine Inheritance."

[10] And He said, "Behold, I make a covenant: before all thy people I will do marvels, such as have not been wrought in all the earth, nor in any nation; and all the people among which thou art shall see the work of Jehovah; for it is a terrible thing that I do with thee."

I wonder how many of us would even discern the difference between an angel going with us, versus the Lord Himself going with us?

I love that description of Moses that the Lord speaks to him face-to-face as to a friend. What level of relationship do you have with the Lord? See Exodus 33:11 and also later in Numbers 12:8 "with him will I speak mouth to mouth, even manifestly, and not in dark speeches;" Isn't this our Heavenly Dad's Heart for us too, to speak with us face-to-face as to a friend?

Family criticism cuts deeply; it's close up and personal. The very personal family criticism outlined in Numbers 12 gives us a wonderful illustration of Moses' heart.

Will this be said of us when those closest to us rise up against us?

> Now the man Moses was very meek, above all the men which were upon the face of the earth. [Numbers 12:3]

Will the Lord Himself say of you and I, as in verses 7 & 8 that we are "faithful in all our house" (all that has been entrusted to us). Will He speak to you "mouth to mouth and not in dark speeches or riddles," verse 8.

Moses did not initiate this move against Aaron and Miriam, in response to their criticism of him—this incident was initiated by the Lord as verse 4 makes very clear. As the three of them are summoned to the tabernacle, the tent of meeting, and Miriam is struck with leprosy. When we are so forcibly vindicated, as Moses was, do we react with arrogance or a haughty self-righteousness? Verse 13 gives us Moses response:

> And Moses cried unto Jehovah, saying, "Heal her, O God, I beseech Thee." [14] And Jehovah said unto Moses, "If her father had but spit in her face, should she not be ashamed seven days? let her be shut up without the camp seven days, and after that she shall be brought in again." [15] And Miriam was shut up without the camp seven days: and the people journeyed not till Miriam was brought in again.

Moving on to Numbers 14 gives us the response to the 12 spies spying out the land.
Numbers 14:6-11:

> And Joshua the son of Nun and Caleb the son of Jephunneh, who were of them that spied out the land, rent their clothes: [7] and they spake unto all the congregation of the children of Israel, saying, "The

land, which we passed through to spy it out, is an exceeding good land. [8] If Jehovah delight in us, then He will bring us into this land, and give it unto us; a land which floweth with milk and honey. [9] Only rebel not against Jehovah, neither fear ye the people of the land; for they are bread for us: their defence is removed from over them, and Jehovah is with us: fear them not." [10] But all the congregation bade stone them with stones. And the Glory of Jehovah appeared in the tent of meeting unto all the children of Israel.

[11] And Jehovah said unto Moses, "How long will this people despise Me? and how long will they not believe in Me, for all the signs which I have wrought among them? [12] I will smite them with the pestilence, and disinherit them, and will make of thee a nation greater and mightier than they."

Oh, how many of us would agree with the Lord over that, but not Moses. Here's a lesson for us in what it means to 'reason with the Lord' as Isaiah describes, Isaiah 1:18. Firstly, here is someone who knows the nature and Heart of the Lord. Secondly, he highlights the Name of the Lord Himself, and how His Reputation is seen and recorded. Thirdly he gives advice to the Lord as to what He should do. Are you in that place of giving the Lord advice? Here, I am again highlighting Moses' reasoning with italics:
Numbers 14:13-19:

And Moses said unto Jehovah, *"Then the Egyptians will hear it; for Thou broughtest up this people in Thy Might from among them;* [14] *and they will tell it to the inhabitants of this land. They have heard that Thou Jehovah art in the midst of this people; for Thou Jehovah art seen face to face, and Thy Cloud standeth over them, and Thou goest before them, in a pillar of cloud by day, and in a pillar of fire by night.* [15] *Now if Thou shalt kill this people as one man, then the nations which have heard the fame of Thee will speak, saying,* [16] *Because Jehovah was not able to bring this people into the land which He sware unto them, therefore He hath slain them in the wilderness.* [17] *And now, I pray Thee, let the Power of the Lord be great, according as Thou hast spoken, saying,* [18] *'Jehovah is slow to anger, and abundant in Lovingkindness, forgiving iniquity and transgression; and that will by no means clear the guilty, visiting the iniquity of the fathers upon the children, upon the third and upon the fourth generation.'* [19] *Pardon, I pray Thee, the iniquity of this people according unto the greatness of Thy Lovingkindness, and according as Thou hast forgiven this people, from Egypt even until now."*

Numbers 16 recounts the rebellion of Korah. In the face of such rebellion directed so specifically against him and Aaron personally, it is indicative of his heart that he doesn't take action himself, but passes the judgment to the Lord to enact:

Numbers 16:28-30:

And Moses said, *"Hereby ye shall know that Jehovah hath sent me to do all these works; for I have* not *done them of mine own mind.* [29] *If these men die the common death of all men, or if they be visited after the visitation of all men; then Jehovah hath not sent me.* [30] *But if Jehovah make a new thing, and the ground open its mouth, and swallow them up, with all that appertain unto them, and they go down alive into Sheol; then ye shall understand that these men have despised Jehovah."*

This was clearly lost on the people, who were all in rebellion mode the following day saying that it was Moses and Aaron who had killed Korah and his family, but here again Moses' heart is revealed:

Numbers 16:42-50:

And it came to pass, when the congregation was assembled against Moses and against Aaron, that they looked toward the tent of meeting: and, behold, the cloud covered it, and the Glory of Jehovah appeared. [43] And Moses and Aaron came to the front of the tent of meeting. [44] And Jehovah spake unto Moses, saying, [45] "Get you up from among this congregation, that I may consume them in a moment." And they fell upon their faces. [46] And Moses said unto Aaron, *"Take thy censer, and put fire therein from off the altar, and lay incense thereon, and carry it quickly unto the congregation, and make atonement for them: for there is wrath gone out from Jehovah; the plague is begun."* [47] And Aaron took as Moses spake, and ran into the midst of the assembly; and, behold, the plague was begun among the people: and he put on the incense, and made atonement for the people. [48] And he stood between the dead and the living; and the plague was stayed. [49] Now they that died by the plague were fourteen thousand and seven hundred, besides them that died about the matter of Korah. [50] And Aaron returned unto Moses unto the door of the tent of meeting: and the plague was stayed."

Numbers 20 recounts another incident that cost Moses his entry to the Promised Land:

Numbers 20:1-13:

> And the children of Israel, even the whole
> congregation, came into the wilderness of Zin in the
> first month: and the people abode in Kadesh; and
> Miriam died there, and was buried there.
> ² And there was no water for the congregation: and
> they assembled themselves together against Moses
> and against Aaron. ³ And the people strove with
> Moses, and spake, saying, "Would that we had died
> when our brethren died before Jehovah! ⁴ And why
> have ye brought the assembly of Jehovah into this
> wilderness, that we should die there, we and our
> beasts? ⁵ And wherefore have ye made us to come up
> out of Egypt, to bring us in unto this evil place? it is
> no place of seed, or of figs, or of vines, or of
> pomegranates; neither is there any water to
> drink." ⁶ And Moses and Aaron went from the
> presence of the assembly unto the door of the tent of
> meeting, and fell upon their faces: and the Glory of
> Jehovah appeared unto them. ⁷ And Jehovah spake
> unto Moses, saying, ⁸ "Take the rod, and assemble
> the congregation, thou, and Aaron thy brother, and
> speak ye unto the rock before their eyes, that it give
> forth its water; and thou shalt bring forth to them
> water out of the rock; so thou shalt give the
> congregation and their cattle drink." ⁹ And Moses
> took the rod from before Jehovah, as he commanded
> him.
> ¹⁰ And Moses and Aaron gathered the assembly
> together before the rock, and he said unto them,
> "Hear now, ye rebels; shall we bring you forth water
> out of this rock?" ¹¹ And Moses lifted up his hand,
> and smote the rock with his rod twice: and water

came forth abundantly, and the congregation drank, and their cattle. ¹² And Jehovah said unto Moses and Aaron, "Because ye believed not in Me, to sanctify Me in the eyes of the children of Israel, therefore ye shall not bring this assembly into the land which I have given them." ¹³ These are the waters of Meribah; because the children of Israel strove with Jehovah, and He was sanctified in them.

Numbers 21 gives us yet another story where the people once again were complaining about Moses taking them out of their slavery in Egypt:

Numbers 21:4-9:

And they journeyed from mount Hor by the way of the Red sea, to compass the land of Edom: and the soul of the people was much discouraged because of the way. ⁵ And the people spake against God, and against Moses, "Wherefore have ye brought us up out of Egypt to die in the wilderness? for there is no bread, neither is there any water; and our soul loatheth this light bread." ⁶ And the Lord sent fiery serpents among the people, and they bit the people; and much people of Israel died. ⁷ Therefore the people came to Moses, and said, "We have sinned, for we have spoken against the Lord, and against thee; pray unto the Lord, that He take away the serpents from us." And Moses prayed for the people. ⁸ And the Lord said unto Moses, "Make thee a fiery serpent, and set it upon a pole: and it shall come to pass, that every one that is bitten, when he looketh upon it, shall live." ⁹ And Moses made a serpent of brass, and put it upon a pole, and it came to pass, that if a serpent had bitten any man, when he beheld the serpent of brass, he lived.

Chapter 11   David, His Anointing and Goliath

King David makes a wonderful illustration for us of how to live as a Covenant Partner to the Lord. There are many lessons we can draw from his life, which will be helpful for us.

David first appears in 1 Samuel 16 when the Lord directs Samuel to go to Bethlehem and anoint one of Jesse's sons as the future king of Israel. As the sons are shown to Samuel, we have the Lord's assessment and reasons for His choice of David recorded there for us. Eliab, the firstborn and most obvious candidate, is called out. The Lord says to Samuel "Do not consider his appearance or his height, for I have rejected him. The Lord does not look at the things people look at. People look at the outward appearance, but the Lord looks at the heart," 1 Samuel 16:7.

So this was David's qualification. As we read further through David's life we need to track what was in David's heart that caused the Lord such delight. There is much there for us.

Concluding this episode, Samuel then goes on and anoints David in the presence of his brothers. From that day on the Spirit of the Lord came powerfully upon him.

So here David is anointed King of Israel, and enters this covenantal relationship with the Lord, though it would be many years between this anointing and its due fulfilment. Clearly this covenantal relationship began with David's being anointed and having the Spirit of the Lord powerfully on him. This had absolutely nothing to do with his outer world, that hadn't changed one bit. Have you been anointed by the Lord? Has Holy Spirit come and powerfully filled you with Himself? Then you have entered that same covenantal partnership—*regardless of any change in your outward circumstances.*

Let's take a look at David's life to see how he lived differently than everyone else, indicative of the relationship he had with the Lord.

It is not specifically given, but David must have grown in his understanding of the power behind this new covenant relationship, well before his confrontation with Goliath. He had already encountered a lion and a bear, so somewhere along this journey he realized something highly significant had changed. This change had evidently gone deeply into his psyche. I'm thinking David must have already developed that relationship with the Lord, before Samuel ever came to anoint him which accounts for how he came to be chosen. Evidently the Lord knew David's heart, to have made David His choice. It makes me wonder what the difference between David and Saul was. Saul was converted into another man when he was anointed to be king by Samuel, 1 Samuel 10:6 & 10. But before that moment, there was no indication that he was looking for a relationship with the Lord. By way of contrast, I strongly suspect that long before his anointing, David had a well developed relationship as a worshipper of the Lord, that he had leaned into out of his own heart, as a child.

When you experience life from the perspective of being a Covenant Partner with the All-Mighty-One, we see things that people otherwise simply don't see. David saw the set-up with Goliath from a completely different perspective than everyone else. He saw Goliath's taunt was not against the army or individuals, but was against the Lord, His Covenant Partner.

When you see your current situation through the eyes of the Lord, from His perspective, then you see something very different to seeing it from the natural perspective.

In his encounter with Goliath, David had a series of serious confrontations. First was with his eldest brother Eliab and such an attack from one's siblings so easily gets deeply under our skin.

See 1 Samuel 17:28:

> When Eliab, David's oldest brother, heard him speaking with the men, he burned with anger at him and asked, "Why have you come down here? And with whom did you leave those few sheep in the wilderness? I know how conceited you are and how wicked your heart is; you came down only to watch the battle."

But look at David's response, verse 29:

> "Now what have I done?" said David. "Can't I even speak?"
>
> Evidently this wasn't the first attack David had had from Eliab!

This is a direct attack on David's character and motives. 'I know how *conceited* you are and how *wicked* your heart'. We scarcely know our own motives let alone those of another! From an elder brother this is truly a two-edged assault.

Next he is confronted by Saul:

1 Samuel 17:32:

> [32] David said to Saul, "Let no one lose heart on account of this Philistine; your servant will go and fight him."
> [33] Saul replied, "You are not able to go out against this Philistine and fight him; you are only a young man, and he has been a warrior from his youth.'"

This is a direct attack on his ability. 'You are *not able*' is attacking his ability, with all of the reasons to back it up. I like David's conclusion, that his own ability is not relevant here, but rather he declares his experience of the Lord, in whom he is trusting:

> [34] But David said to Saul, "Your servant has been keeping his father's sheep. When a lion or a bear came and carried off a sheep from the flock, [35] I went after it, struck it and rescued the sheep from its mouth. When it turned on me, I seized it by its hair, struck it and killed it. [36] Your servant has killed both the lion and the bear; this uncircumcised Philistine will be like one of them, because he has defied the armies of the living God. [37] The Lord who rescued me from the paw of the lion and the paw of the bear will rescue me from the hand of this Philistine."

1 Samuel 17:38-39:

> And Saul armed David with his armour, and he put an helmet of brass upon his head; also he armed him with a coat of mail. And David girded his sword upon his armour, and he assayed to go; for he had not proved it. And David said unto Saul, "I cannot go in these, because I am not used to them." So he took them off. Then he took his staff in his hand, chose five smooth stones from the stream, put them in the pouch of his shepherd's bag and, with his sling in his hand, approached the Philistine.

Don't fight the enemy's battles on his terms, with his weapons. Fight with the weapons you are familiar with and expert in, on your terms, with the Lord's guidance and anointing. The weapons of our warfare aren't physical, natural weapons, or you're fighting the wrong battle, 2 Corinthians 10:4! So what spiritual weapons are you familiar and expert in, such as worship, remembering and applying Bible verses so praying scripture, receiving prophetic words or insights or visions?

Author and teacher, Dutch Sheets, points out that it is probable that David's staff would have been engraved with the lion and the bear, displaying his history.

The next verses describe David's confrontation with Goliath.

1 Samuel 17:41-44:

> Meanwhile, the Philistine, with his shield-bearer in front of him, kept coming closer to David. He looked David over and saw that he was little more than a boy, glowing with health and handsome, and he despised him. He said to David, "Am I a dog, that you come at me with sticks?" And the Philistine cursed David by his gods. "Come here," he said, "and I'll give your flesh to the birds and the wild animals!"

This is a direct attack against David's God and, effectively, his covenant with his God. Verse 26 reveals David's mindset:

> "Who is this uncircumcised Philistine that he should defy the armies of the Living God?"

To refer to Goliath as "an uncircumcised Philistine" is underlining that Goliath has no covenant relationship with God, as circumcision was the key to that covenant. David, on the other hand, did have just the kind of covenant relationship that was needed here.

Moving on to 1 Samuel 17:45-47:

> David said to the Philistine, "You come against me with sword and spear and javelin, but I come against you in the name of the Lord Almighty, the God of the armies of Israel, whom you have defied. This day

the Lord will deliver you into my hands, and I'll strike you down and cut off your head. This very day I will give the carcasses of the Philistine army to the birds and the wild animals, and the whole world will know that there is a God in Israel. All those gathered here will know that it is not by sword or spear that the Lord saves; for the battle is the Lord's, and He will give all of you into our hands."

Our covenant relationship impacts our *character and motives*, it impacts our *ability* and it impacts our *relationship* with our Heavenly Dad.

1 Samuel 18 sets down what happens when this anointing and favour from God is seen by all. Everyone speaks well of David and he succeeds at everything he is asked to do. But the effect makes King Saul deeply jealous. When the authority to whom you have to answer, sees and recognises the anointing and favour resting on you, it can highlight their deficiency causing jealousy. But this places a very different set of constraints upon David that he carries masterfully—*he stays humble*. So often such favour and blessing goes straight to our heads. Many would say this is the hardest season to navigate!

Earlier, Saul had offered his daughter to whoever killed Goliath. Sometime after David's victory, Saul rather belatedly does offer David his elder daughter Merab. 1 Samuel 18:18 records David's response:

"Who am I and what is my family or clan in Israel, that I should become the king's son-in-law?" So Saul gave Merab in marriage to Adriel of Meholah."

Just as Abram's and Moses's relationship with the Lord had to grow, so too did David's and so too does ours. The responsibilities of being a Covenant Partner aren't dropped on us on day one. We are expected to grow in favour, relationship and understanding with the Lord, and that has to include understanding the responsibilities and privileges of our role as a Covenant Partner. This is very analogous to the growth of a child and their responsibilities and privileges within the family.

A little appendix to this chapter:

But what we readily miss in this story is 1 Samuel 18:20, that Michal, Merab's younger sister, was in love with David, which pleased Saul who arranged for David to marry her instead. This is a curious twist to the event that we all remember from 2 Samuel 6 that occurred much later when Michal looking through a window, saw David leaping and dancing before the Lord as they brought the Ark of the Covenant to Jerusalem next to David's palace, and she despises David in her heart.

2 Samuel 6:20-23:

Then David returned to bless his household. And Michal the daughter of Saul came out to meet David, and said, How glorious was the king of Israel today, who uncovered himself to day in the eyes of the handmaids of his servants, as one of the vain fellows shamelessly uncovereth himself!

21 And David said unto Michal, It was before the Lord, which chose me before thy father, and before all his house, to appoint me ruler over the people of the Lord, over Israel: therefore will I play before the Lord.

22 And I will yet be more vile than thus, and will be base in mine own sight: and of the maidservants which thou hast spoken of, of them shall I be had in honor.

23 Therefore Michal the daughter of Saul had no child unto the day of her death.

Chapter 12   David's Honor and Respect for the Anointing

As we go further into David's life I need to draw out the principles and leave you, the reader, to work your way through the verses.

These principles of walking out a life as a Covenant Partner are repeated and repeated throughout David's life—we do well to note them, and follow them!

1/ Respect and honor the Lord's anointing.
See 2 Samuel 7:18 and 1 Chronicles 17:16.

2/ Respect and honor those He has anointed.
See Matthew 10:41, "He who receives a prophet, receives a prophet's reward."

3/ Respect and honor those in authority for the position's sake if you are unable to honor the person holding that office. Saul was God's anointed King who David honored even while for years Saul hunted him down to kill him.
See 1 Samuel 26:24, "As surely as I valued your life today, so may the Lord value my life and deliver me from all trouble."

4/ Never retaliate against those set against you or cursing you, 2 Samuel 16:5-13, and extend ready forgiveness to them, as in 2 Samuel 19:16-23 which may be even harder.

5/ Honor others, especially those who have helped or recognised you.
2 Samuel 19:31-38. Note how Barzillai had provided for David when he was kicked off the throne and on the wrong side of the Jordan, see 2 Samuel 17:27-29.

6/ Don't take the law into your own hands, however bad the injustice looks: 1 Samuel 25.

This could be rewritten as Honor the Lord, by letting Him bring His Justice to bear, not yours.

What sums this up and sums up so much of David's life?
Honor, Honor and more Honor.

If you value the anointing Holy Spirit has placed on your life, then guard and honor the anointing well, wherever you see it. One vital key here is to guard that relationship with Holy Spirit who makes that anointing possible. Another is to look out for, and respect the anointing on others. This can be difficult when their anointing is very very different to yours, or when it is so similar they are treading on your toes. As I have mentioned already, "He who receives a prophet, receives a prophet's reward," Matthew 10:41.

David always refused to kill King Saul though he had many opportunities as King Saul hunted him down. The first occasion is recounted in 1 Samuel 24 when Saul inadvertently goes in to the very cave where David and his men are hiding. David cuts off the bottom of Saul's kingly robe, but afterwards "David's heart smote him, because he had cut off Saul's robe, Verse 5." From a safe distance, David holds up the piece he has cut off and confronts Saul. He declares, "The Lord judge between me and thee, and the Lord avenge me of thee: but mine hand shall not be upon thee" Verse 12. We have to remember here that Saul had come out with three thousand chosen men for the sole purpose of finding and killing David. David's heart is not lost on Saul, who acknowledges "Thou art more righteous than I: for thou hast rewarded me good," verse 17, and "Now I know well that thou shalt surely be king and that the kingdom of Israel shall be established in thine hand," verse 20.

This didn't stop Saul from seeking to kill David. David's motivation is further revealed in his second major opportunity to kill Saul, given to us in 1 Samuel 26:23-24:

The Lord rewards everyone for their righteousness and faithfulness. The Lord delivered you into my hands today, but I would not lay a hand on the Lord's anointed. *As surely as I valued your life today, so may the Lord value my life and deliver me from all trouble."* (NIV)   [Italics mine.]

This is a respect for the one who Father God had anointed, for the anointing, and for the position that they represent. David had long since lost all respect for Saul as a person, but he respected and honored Saul as the anointed King. He recognised that the kingship required and carried its own special anointing. David knew all too well that one day he would be in that position himself. We would do well to recognise that today with those in authority. For those with the eyes to see, that anointing was lacking on Absalom when he usurped David and stole the Kingship.

We really need to look out for, respect and recognise the Holy Spirit anointing on another, especially the unlikely ones. In many ways this is the simple lesson of treating others as you would like to be treated—would you like people to see and recognise the anointing that you carry?

When those coming to tell David of the death of his enemies, to say they killed them, David commands them to be killed for touching those who the Lord had anointed:
2 Samuel 1:12-14:

And they mourned, and wept, and fasted until even, for Saul, and for Jonathan his son, and for the people of the Lord, and for the house of Israel; because they were fallen by the sword.
13 And David said unto the young man that told him, Whence art thou? And he answered, I am the son of a stranger, an Amalekite.

¹⁴ And David said unto him, "How wast thou not afraid to stretch forth thine hand to destroy the Lord's anointed?"
¹⁵ And David called one of the young men, and said, "Go near, and fall upon him." And he smote him that he died.
¹⁶ And David said unto him, "Thy blood be upon thy head; for thy mouth hath testified against thee, saying, I have slain the Lord's anointed."
¹⁷ And David lamented with this lamentation over Saul and over Jonathan his son. (KJV)

David repeated this, ordering Rechab and Baanah to be killed for their murder of Ishbosheth, Saul's remaining son in 2 Samuel 4: 7-12.

How much more, when wicked men have slain a righteous person in his own house upon his bed? Shall I not therefore now require his blood of your hand? (KJV)   2 Samuel 4:11

Giving place to, and honoring those whom the Lord has anointed in past seasons, is completely counter to our modern ways of thinking. How readily we criticise and kill with our words those who carried a wonderful anointing from the Lord and for whatever reason have dropped it and maybe even now running counter to what the Lord is doing in this season. Remember Saul was hunting David down to kill him for many years, but David refused to touch him. He was always wanting to honor that Holy Spirit Anointing. We do well to follow! If we have nothing good to say, then we are better off keeping quiet than carping or criticising.

With the imminent new wave of anointing and our Heavenly Dad's move across the earth, things will be different and look different. Many of those who were anointed in the last move, or in the current move, will struggle with the differences between what they are comfortable with and what they see sweeping through. Many will oppose and criticise the new, and somehow we have to honor and respect them while ignoring their criticism, and pressing on with the Lord's new agenda and new way of doing things. He will be revealing new facets of who He is, and what and how He wants to work among us, and us to co-labour with Him.

Honor others, particularly those who have helped or recognised you:

2 Samuel 2:4-7:

David honoring those who buried Saul.

2 Samuel 3:10-27:

David honoring Abner who had stood by Saul, and finally brought the 11 remaining tribes under David's kingship.

2 Samuel 9, the whole chapter.

David honoring the covenant he had cut with Jonathan.

Watch over your words to fulfil your promises and words to others. This can be costly.

Next—don't take the law into your own hands. It is so easy to judge others, and we want to rush out and execute judgment—and we do just that with our words oh so readily, even if we don't with our fists or a gun.

We have the story of Nabal and Abigail in 1 Samuel 25. David and his men have been covering Nabal's flocks and herd and herdsmen, but when it's festival time, David's men are treated rudely invoking David's intent with his men to take the law into his own hands and slaughter (murder) Nabal's house. Fortunately Abigail, Nabal's wife rushes to make amends and see David and his men are appropriately provided for.

Look at the sense of injustice here, that burned in David's heart, but it was vitally important that the Lord vindicated him and that David didn't do what he had intended. The Lord brought the judgment, without David or his men doing anything. This is a tough lesson for us to learn! David so nearly missed it here.

The Lord's Kingdom is Righteousness on a foundation of justice, and as He floods our lives with Himself, He heightens our sense of justice and injustice. But right in the face of that we have to watch this principle and that we don't take the law into our own hands. Let the Lord Himself be the judge. "Vengeance is mine, I will repay, says the Lord," Deuteronomy 32:35.

These are not easy lessons to learn and not easily carried through. This is the cost of carrying the Lord's anointing. It demands that we stay close to Him, drinking deeply of His Heart and Spirit, Romans 11:29.

Chapter 13   Learn how to build yourself up in the Lord

There will always be times when everything around you is screaming that you have failed and that the Lord is not going to come through for you. Each of us has to learn how we as individuals can come back into the Lord's presence and confirm and strengthen our relationship with Him before moving on again. We have His promise that, "He will never leave us or forsake us," Hebrews 13:5. In these situations we need to take time out to re-establish that relationship, His Presence and Anointing in us. This is not a promise to lightly assume.

In John 10:22-42, after a bruising encounter with the Jews in the temple as to whether or not He was indeed the Messiah, Jesus left and went to where John had baptized Him, and rested there. He went back to where Father had so specifically confirmed His identity with that word spoken to Him, "You are my beloved son, in whom, I am well pleased." It was there that news came of Lazarus being sick, but He continued to stay there two more days. If Jesus needed to take time out like this, then how much more, on occasion, do we need to do the same?

And there is a corollary to this. We always have to move from a place of relationship. There is a huge need to wait and receive the Lord's direction for the next step. It is highly dangerous to assume that what worked last time is what or how the Lord intends to move again. He loves variety, so while the end objective may be the same as before, the route to getting there is almost certainly going to be different. Remember this cost Moses his entry into the Promised Land! (See Numbers 20:10:13, see page 75-76.)

These facets come out of the next story of David in 1 Samuel 30 with the destruction of David's place at Ziklag by the Amalekites. Curiously this was when David and his men had left Ziklag to fight the Israelites with the Philistine army—recounted in chapter 29. 1 Samuel 30 recounts their return to Ziklag to find it destroyed by fire and their wives and sons and daughters taken captive.

1 Samuel 30:6 (NIV):

> David was greatly distressed because the men were talking of stoning him; each was bitter in spirit because of his sons and daughters. *But David found strength in the Lord his God.* (Italics mine)

So David took time out and knew how to turn to the Lord and re-establish his relationship with Him.

He called Abiathar the priest to ask the Lord what to do—whether to pursue the attackers.

1 Samuel 30:8 The answer was:

> Pursue them, you will certainly overtake them and you will recover everyone and everything.

So here David is showing his trust and reliance on the Lord—not himself. How easy in this situation to gather everyone and with human charisma pull everyone's grief into rage and set off in pursuit. This is not David's way, but to ask the Lord first.

His men were tired and by the time they reached the Besor valley, two hundred of his six hundred men were simply too exhausted to go any further. Only four hundred of his men were able to carry on with David.

1 Samuel 30:16 onwards tells us that they finally caught up with the attackers eating and drinking and celebrating, and fought them from dusk until evening of the

following day. They recovered everything they had lost—nothing was missing. David brought everything back with him driving the flocks and herds ahead of them. But when they reached the two hundred who had been too tired to cross the Besor valley trouble erupted, 1 Samuel 30:21.

1 Samuel 30:22-25 (NIV):

> All the evil men and troublemakers among David's followers said, "Because they did not go out with us, we will not share with them the plunder we recovered. However, each man may take his wife and children and go.
>
> 23 David replied, "'No my brothers, you must not do that with what the Lord has given us. He has protected us and delivered into our hands the raiding party that came against us. 24 Who will listen to what you say? The share of the men who stayed with the supplies is to be the same as that of him who went to the battle. All will share alike!" 25 *David made this a statute and ordinance for Israel unto this day.*

So here in the midst of the elation of victory and vindication is a righteous clear-headed judgment. And this was so recognised it became a mandate for generations to follow, us included.

David then went on to send gifts of the plunder to the elders of Judah and to other places where he and his men had roamed (verses 27-30). Here we see David's generosity.

***   ***   ***

1 Samuel 31 recounts the battle with the Philistines where Saul and his three sons were all killed. Moving on to 2 Samuel 2, and contemplating whether now, with Saul finally dead, was the time to take up the kingship for which he had

been anointed all those years ago, David still doesn't 'assume' anything, but goes back to question the Lord.

2 Samuel 2:1 (NIV):

> In the course of time, David inquired of the Lord. "Shall I go up to one of the towns of Judah?" he asked.
>
> The Lord said, "Go up."
>
> David asked, "Where shall I go?"
>
> "To Hebron," the Lord answered.

It is only in 2 Samuel Chapter 5 that David is finally anointed king over all Israel, seven years six months after the start of his reign over Judah. And his reign over all Israel lasted for 33 years (2 Samuel 5:5).

Needless to say there were more wars with the Philistines. 2 Samuel 5:17-20 recounts the first war, after David had been anointed king over all Israel. The Philistines went out in full force to find him. David's first action, as always, was to inquire of the Lord.

2 Samuel 5:19-21 (NIV):

> Shall I go and attack the Philistines? Will you deliver them into my hands?
>
> The Lord answered him, "Go, for I will surely deliver the Philistines into your hands." [20] "So David went to Baal Perazim, and there he defeated them. He said, "As waters break out, the Lord has broken out against my enemies before me." So that place was called Baal Perazim. [21] The Philistines abandoned their idols there, and David and his men carried them off.

In Vs 22 the Philistines tried again, and once more David inquired of the Lord:

2 Samuel 5:23-25 (NIV):

> And He answered, "Do not go straight up, but circle around behind them and attack them in front of the poplar trees. [24] As soon as you hear the sound of marching in the tops of the poplar trees, move quickly, because that will mean the Lord has gone out in front of you to strike the Philistine army." [25] So David did as the Lord commanded him, and he struck down the Philistines from Gibeon to Gezer.

The key principles boil down to:

Honor: Holy Spirit—and
those He has anointed
those who have helped you and recognised your worth.

Relationship: Learn how to build and maintain that intimate relationship with the Lord.
Don't assume anything, but wait for and listen to the Lord's instructions.

Generosity: Especially to those who have been generous to you.

Worship: True worship flows out of experience in relationship with the Lord.

Chapter 14   David the King

There are many different facets of David's kingship that illustrate the anointing he lived under. As I have shown, he had learned the need to build up his own spirit and encourage himself in the Lord. With increased responsibility comes the increased need to build up one's spirit, to honor, lean on and draw on that anointing. I will illustrate just a few here.

Although anointed to be king by Samuel years earlier, he never presumes on this. And even when recognised and anointed king over Judah at Hebron, 2 Samuel 2:4, he bides his time to be recognised by the other tribes. He doesn't force his kingship on others, but trusts in the Lord to set him over the whole of Israel. He was king over Judah only, for seven years six months before the elders of the other tribes came and made a league with him in Hebron anointing him king over all Israel, 2 Samuel 5:3.

Once again, even when one of his sons, Absalom, forces him out in a coup, David doesn't force his kingship on others, but trusts the Lord to set him in that place. He is most concerned over Absalom's life in the ensuing conflict, 2 Samuel 18:5. And as David leaves Jerusalem, fleeing for his life, he doesn't return cursing with cursing, 2 Samuel 16:5-13. We may not be king, but we are lord over some aspects of our world. Are we slaving away over our rights? Or are we like Jesus, who came to serve:

> Although He was God, didn't see this as something to hold onto, but laid it aside…. He took on not just human form, but that of a servant with His mind, will and spirit totally aligned with His Father's.
> Philippians 2:6 & 7   *L & B Translation*

The moment David is king he seeks the Ark, the Presence of God, and His Glory. He wants it as close to his own dwelling as he can get. This had been entirely neglected during Saul's reign. David knew he needed time in the Lord's Presence.

David broke the rules of the Old Covenant by setting up the tabernacle (tent) for the Ark, right next to the palace and would approach the Ark closely. Some scholars say he put the Ark on a table so that he could lie underneath it and look up at the wings of the angelic cherubim outstretched from its lid. It would be very natural from this place of worship encounter, that he would write expressions like we find in Psalm 91:4, "He covers me with His mighty pinions, and under His wings I will take refuge. His Truth is my shield and buckler." Here was a place of safety from the snares of men, from pestilence, from fear by night, the arrow by day, and destruction at noon. Here was his secret place where he could lie under the shadow of the Almighty, Psalm 91:1-7.

He honored his word and his earlier covenant with Jonathan. When David was firmly established as king in 2 Samuel 9:1 he enquired whether there were any descendents left of Saul's son, Jonathan, his covenant partner. Jonathan, as Saul's son would be the natural heir, and any surviving son of Jonathan would then be his heir, so would be a threat to David's kingship. Instead, David invites Mephibosheth to dine alongside his own sons at his own table, effectively becoming one of his own family.

He learned those early lessons well, especially to not take vengeance and the lives of others, into his own hands, which he so nearly did with Nabal in 1 Samuel 25:2-29. When someone came claiming to have killed Saul in 2 Samuel 1:10, expecting to be rewarded for killing David's nemesis, David promptly commands one of those standing by to kill the guy for killing the Lord's anointed, 1 Samuel 1:14-16. When Joab and Abishai kill Saul's major general Abner, because he had slain their brother Asahel, David very publicly laments the death of this great man, making it very clear this wasn't his heart or intent, 2 Samuel 3:33-39.

He trusted the Lord and sought His Way and His Solution, rather than simply repeating what had worked before, or relying on his own perceived strength. In 2 Samuel 5:19 when the Philistines come against him, he enquires of the Lord before simply going up against them. And when they come against him for a second time in 2 Samuel 5:22-25, as I mentioned at the end of the previous chapter, the Lord gives him a completely different strategy.

He prepared for Solomon to become king in his place. Interleaved in the pages of Proverbs it is clear Solomon was schooled to be king after David, such as Proverbs 1:8, and Proverbs 4:3 & 4. He publicly declared Solomon to be king after him in 1 Chronicles 28:5 and gives some wonderful instructions for his kingship, 1 Chronicles 28:9. Then in 1 Kings 1 he took the necessary steps, with Bathsheba, Solomon's mother, and Nathan the prophet, to see that outworked. 1 Kings 1 is a fascinating chapter, showing how he orders the transition, illustrating his kingly authority even in his final moments.

He prepares—he prepares for Solomon to build the temple he had dreamed of. It is to his design and he laid up much of the material: 1 Chronicles 28. He gives Solomon very clear instructions,

> Consider this carefully, for the Lord has chosen you
> to build a house for the sanctuary. Be courageous and
> strong and do it,. (AMP)   1 Chronicles 28:10

Then he outlines the design and plans in 1 Chronicles 9-19, that the Lord had given to him.

What preparations can we make for those coming after us? What plans, what instructions, what provisions, what advice?

When David falls, he is completely oblivious of the depth of evil into which he had sunk. When Nathan comes with his story, David is completely unaware that the story is about himself. How readily success, fame and fortune can blind and deceive us. One of the problems of deception, by its very nature, is we are unable to see it in ourselves.

2 Samuel 12:5 (NIV):

> David burned with anger against the man and said to Nathan, "As surely as the Lord lives, the man who did this must die!"
>
> [7] Then Nathan said to David, "You are the man! This is what the Lord, the God of Israel, says: 'I anointed you king over Israel, and I delivered you from the hand of Saul. [8] I gave your master's house to you, and your master's wives into your arms. I gave you all Israel and Judah. And if all this had been too little, I would have given you even more.'"

But note the depth of David's repentance and how he waits before the Lord until he knows he is forgiven, Psalm 51.

Chapter 15   David the Worshipper

David loved the Presence of the Lord and brought His Presence, symbolised by the Ark of the Covenant, as close as he could get it to his own palace, and instituted continual worship there.

[Note that in 2 Samuel 6:12 The Lord blessed Obed-Edom and everything he has—while the Ark is left in his house. David wanted in on that himself.]

David was an outrageous public worshipper of the Lord, 2 Samuel 6:16 & 22. His dancing and worship wasn't hidden away, but right out at the front of the procession. This is still offensive today to those with no relationship with the Lord, just as it was offensive to his wife Michal.

He missed it with his affair with Bathsheba and murder of Bathsheba's husband Uriah, see 2 Samuel 11, all because he wasn't out fighting when he should have been.

He then sent Uriah to his death to cover his own tracks, see 2 Samuel 11:14. But note his repentant response when confronted by Nathan, see 2 Samuel 12:13.

David knew what it was to be forgiven, see Psalm 51, and 2 Samuel 12:15-23, as did the apostle Paul, who murdered many of those early believers. Can you say, like Paul, that you have wronged no-one as in 2 Corinthians 7:2, because you know your sin has been totally dealt with and blotted out, as in Colossians 2:14?

David was a genuine worshipper of the Lord. He wrote many of the Psalms which covered many different seasons of his life, as well as his varied, and often testing, life experiences. What is noticeable about David's Psalms is that he always ends in a position of faith and trust, often clearly leaning and drawing on his Covenant with the Lord.

For example Psalm 13 begins with:
> How long, Lord? Will you forget me forever? How long will you hide Your face from me?

But it ends with:
> But I trust in Your Unfailing Love; my heart rejoices in Your Salvation. I will sing the Lord's Praise, for He has been good to me.

Compare this to Psalm 44 where mention is made of that Covenant, but there is no drawing upon that relationship with faith and trust:

Psalm 44:
> [15] I live in disgrace all day long, and my face is covered with shame [16] at the taunts of those who revile me, because of the enemy, who is bent on revenge. [17] All this came upon us, though we had not forgotten You; we had not been false to Your covenant. [18] Our hearts had not turned back; our feet had not strayed from Your Path.

> There is a self-righteousness in verses 17 and 18, and a forgetting of that eternal truth that "without faith it is impossible to please God" Hebrews 11:16. "And that He is a rewarder of them that diligently seek Him."

Now see how Psalm 44 ends:

Psalm 44:
> [24] Why do you hide Your Face and forget our misery and oppression? [25] We are brought down to the dust; our bodies cling to the ground. [26] Rise up and help us; rescue us because of Your Unfailing Love.

> Clearly this wasn't written by David.

> Many Christians know of the Lord's Covenant Promises, but never pray in faith and trust for that Covenant

Assistance, but rather lean on and rely on the Lord's Character, and Nature. The whole intent of Covenant is for it to be legally binding upon both parties. It is intended to undergird our whole relationship to reinforce our faith and trust, with that extra security.

David set up a tent around the Ark of the Covenant, for continual worship as though living in our New Covenant era rather than the Old Covenant era. Under the Mosaic law, only the High Priest could come into the Holy of Holies where the Ark of the Covenant was, and even then only once per year. Evidently David and his worship teams went freely in and out. There is no record of them putting on priestly garments, which if they weren't priests then they weren't entitled to wear anyway. There's no record of his tent of worship having all of the "normal tent of meeting" items as had been directed by Moses, and described in Exodus 25, and set out in Exodus 26 such as the table with the Shew Bread, the Laver, and the seven-branched golden lampstand the Menorah. The inference from 1 Kings 3:4 is that these were set up in Gibeon.

So David prioritised the Ark with the Presence of the Lord, over and above the form that was set up in Gibeon. Note that it was in Gibeon the Lord appeared to Solomon in a dream by night: and God said, "ask what shall I give thee". When Solomon awoke he hurried back to Jerusalem.
1 Kings 3:15:

> And stood before the ark of the covenant of the Lord, and offered up burnt offerings, and offered peace offerings, and made a feast to all his servants

Solomon knew exactly where the Presence of the Lord was, and where to sacrifice his thank offerings.

How do you personally, in your own walk with the Lord, prioritize the Lord's Presence over and above the Forms of Christianity?

It was in David's heart to build a temple, 2 Samuel 7:2. I love it that he says to Nathan that he wants to build a house for the Lord. But straightaway in 2 Samuel 7:4-17 Nathan comes back with the word that rather, the Lord wants to build David a house—his descendants forever on the throne.

Then David goes and sits before the Lord and pours out his thankful heart. There is an ease displayed here in his relationship with the Lord—he sits down. His words are humble and awestruck. I personally love this chapter. This is not the prayer of a New Covenant believer—this is 1000 years before Jesus!

2 Samuel 7:18-29 (NIV):

> 18 "Who am I, Sovereign Lord, and what is my family, that you have brought me this far?
>
> 19 "And as if this were not enough in Your Sight, Sovereign Lord, You have also spoken about the future of the house of Your Servant—and this decree, Sovereign Lord, is for a mere human!
>
> 20 "What more can David say to You? For You know Your Servant, Sovereign Lord. For the sake of Your Word and according to Your Will, you have done this great thing and made it known to Your Servant.
>
> 22 "How great You are, Sovereign Lord! There is no one like You, and there is no God but You, as we have heard with our own ears. And who is like Your People Israel—the one nation on earth that God went out to redeem as a people for Himself, and to make a name for Himself, and to perform great and awesome wonders by driving out nations and their gods from

before Your People, whom You redeemed from Egypt? You have established Your People Israel as Your very own for ever, and You, Lord, have become their God.

[25] "And now, Lord God, keep for ever the promise You have made concerning Your Servant and his house. Do as You promised, so that Your Name will be great for ever. Then people will say, 'The Lord Almighty is God over Israel!' And the house of Your Servant David will be established in Your Sight.

[27] "Lord Almighty, God of Israel, You have revealed this to Your Servant, saying, 'I will build a house for you.' So Your Servant has found courage to pray this prayer to You. Sovereign Lord, You are God! Your Covenant is trustworthy, and You have promised these good things to Your Servant. Now be pleased to bless the house of Your Servant, that it may continue for ever in Your Sight; for You, Sovereign Lord, have spoken, and with Your Blessing the house of Your Servant will be blessed for ever."

As the Lord's Covenant Partners we also need to be worshippers. How high is worship in your priorities and use of time?

How freely do you enter His Courts with Praise and High Praise to the King of ALL Kings?

How freely do you express yourself in your praise, and in your worship to Him?

In tongues

In new songs, of the moment

With laughter

With tears

In dance with all of your body reflecting your spirit

With flags or other instruments of expression of worship, such as a shofar or tambourine

Prostrate in awe before Him

Sitting with Him, resting, and enjoying His Presence—with thankfulness.

Chapter 16   Covenant Celebration

It was at the Last Supper that Jesus, with His disciples, cut covenant with Father God. This was then sealed with the sacrifice of Himself on the cross.

His simple request to His disciples was for them to repeat this in His memory.

Communion is not some religious ritual throwback from archaic religious denominations. It is a covenant re-enactment. One of the key aspects of a covenant is its memorial, and here we have the memorial of the initiation of this Covenant between God and Man. A covenant passes down the generations, so what was cut by Jesus, was cut on our behalf, and the power and strength if this covenant continues today.

So when you or I need access to this Covenant then all we have to do is to re-enact this memorial, and take your request to Father God—take His promise back to Him. And He expects this of us. In John 16:23 Jesus told His Disciples, in the context of living out this covenant that they had just entered into, that they wouldn't go to Him with their requests, but directly to the Father. But remember that this is a reciprocal binding relationship, so He may well make a similar request on you. This is not to be entered into lightly.

All the power and strength of the covenant participant legally stands behind their covenant. No wonder then that Paul writes,

> 27 Whoever participates in this breaking of bread and drinking this cup—in this celebration of this Covenant with the Lord, Father God, and does so unworthily and disrespectfully, is guilty of being

disrespectful to the Body and Blood of the Lord Jesus and hence of Father God Himself.

^{28} So each one of you needs to search his heart first, as to his relationship with Father God and this Covenant Jesus made with Father on our behalf, on your behalf, and only then participate. To participate when there are issues between you and Him, makes you guilty of being disrespectful to this Covenant sealed by the Body and Blood of Jesus the Lord.

^{30} *This is why many of you are ill, sick and some have even died* [because you didn't draw on the covenant that you were signing up to by participating].

1 Corinthians 11:27-30:   *L & B Translation*

A full breakdown of this memorial is given in my earlier book '*Mercy—God's Covenant Assistance.*'

Chapter 17   Intimacy

This is all about relationship. Your classic evangelist will, quite justifiably, be most concerned as to whether you have received Jesus as your personal Saviour and made Him your Lord—so that you know Jesus. Jesus chases us down through life's circumstances until we choose to make Him the Lord of our heart and life. But that is so much more than simply praying the sinner's prayer!

We almost miss that Jesus taught that there was something even more important. In Matthew 7, Jesus describes a moment when He is separating those who will enter His Kingdom, and those who won't: Matt 7:22, "Many will say to me in that day, 'Lord, Lord have we not prophesied in Thy Name? And in Thy Name have cast out devils? And in Thy Name done many wonderful works?' [23]And then will I profess unto them, 'I never knew you: depart from Me ye that work iniquity.'" (KJV) So while it is just so important that we know Jesus, *it is even more important that He knows us*!

John in Revelation 3:20 puts it this way, "Behold I stand at the door and knock: if any man hears My Voice, and opens the door, I will come in to him, and will sup with him and he with Me." (KJV) Remember this wasn't written to unbelievers, but to the believers in Laodicea.

So this does beg the question, "How well does He know you?" It is one thing to know all about you, but quite another to have met you, befriended you, and know what makes you tick.

Jesus is knocking, but we have to invite Him into our hearts and our thoughts. Now if you or I were God, wouldn't we simply blow the door off its hinges—just who does this person think they are? But He is not like that—He never invades our personal privacy. He waits patiently for us to open up to invite Him in, and He wants to spend time with us, to sit down for a meal with us. In that culture, to have a meal with someone was a very intimate thing.

If we are coming to someone's house for the first time, or if you are looking round with the possibility of living in it, then we are shown round, room by room. Will you show Jesus around your heart and life, room by room? Can He be trusted? Just how well do you know Him? There are very few people who I am open with and there's much that I don't share even with them. So have you learned openness and trust with the King-of-all-Kings? Have you learned that when He looks into your heart and soul, He searches deeply? I may well try to explain and tell you that He doesn't search to condemn, but to bring life, wholeness and healing. Do you *know* that deeply inside where it matters?

To *know* Him, is to love Him! To know Him is to yearn for Him to be Lord, not just of our external world, but of our internal world also. But such openness also takes courage, and an open and trusting spirit. So, do you pull down the shutters quickly or stay, gazing into His Eyes. As you gaze into His Heart, He is looks into yours. It is in these very moments when He exposes His to you. Sometimes this is easier to do than at other times.

King David described this wonderfully in Psalm 139, evidence that He knew intimacy with the Lord like few others. Can you, like him, say "Search me, O God, and know my heart: try me, and know my thoughts!"? Psalm 139: 23.

Chapter 18   Psalm 139

Dare I look into Your eyes, King Jesus?

One look and I know You have seen right through me, right through all my pretences, and pretensions. You see everything I do; nothing can be hidden from You. And yet my eyes are drawn back to Your deep, deep wells of love, and to let You see into the very depths of who and what I am. Thank You that You don't violate my privacy, and the privacy of my internal world.

Thank You, Lord that there's no guilt or shame in Your look of love for me, no disappointment or hurt as You see and understand my thoughts and my heart. Thank You that I sense only a love that draws me to You and yearns for You to come and search out my heart, my motives, my longings, my loves. *Oh,* come and bring Your love, and Your wholeness to the broken places, Your peace to the fractured, and Your Joy to my heart.

Lord, I give You all my ways, I want to open all of my heart to You, as if I really could hide anything anyway. For You know what I'm about to say before I've even formed the words. You formed and shaped me with such a loving touch from Your hand, Lord, the magnitude and detail of Your loving care is incredible; it's far too big for me to get my head around.

Where can I hide from You and Holy Spirit? I'm having a hard time thinking why I would want to right now, but there are times when I'm hurt and angry and lashing out...You are still close. If I go and take a ride in the International Space Station, You'll still be there with me, and I seem to remember that You made quite an impact on those who went to the moon. If I drop down in some underwater capsule to the depths and darkness of the Pacific Ocean, I won't have left

You behind. Similarly if I jet off into the sunrise and set up home on some distant island, that gentle tender touch of Your loving hand will never be far away, and Your right hand will never let go.

If I think to myself that surely some blackout curtains can turn the day into night, and You'll never be able to see me, then even when I can't see my own finger in front of my face, it will still be as bright as day to You.

Oh my King Jesus, just how did You create me in my mother's womb? You really are amazing, how You formed each part of my anatomy so uniquely, and my soul and spirit too. Even identical twins have such unique souls and spirits; they're still totally unique to You. Just how do You do that Lord? *Oh,* everything You do is so wonderful; that has to be pretty obvious to everyone with eyes to see! All Praise and Glory to You!

Thank You that I wasn't an accident and hidden from You as I was coming together, but rather You had Your creative hand of genius putting me together totally in secret. You saw those cells growing and multiplying and already You had all my days written in the Lamb's book of Life—Wow!

Oh Papa God, all Your thoughts for me, they're so precious, so good, so big! And so many I could never count them if I tried, way more than the grains of sand on every seashore. When I stop my dreaming and wake up, *Oh, Oh,* thank You,. my King, You're still with me and thinking of me.

Oh that my thoughts were like that, Lord. You know the bloodthirsty, selfish, angry, proud thoughts that assail my mind inside, like my enemies outside who despise Your name, "Jesus". *Oh,* You know how I hate them both, Lord. You know how I am so easily ensnared and seduced by their train of thought, and entertain them far longer than I should. *Oh,* how I hate them, and how they pollute my thought life.

Lord, search me. Lord, come in and walk with me through every aspect of my heart and life. Lord, I *want* You to know me, to know me better than I know myself. I want You to show me anything that displeases You—anything, Lord.

Lord, I can't change me, but *You* can change me. So Holy Spirit, show me and help me tend the garden of my heart with Your royal care. Help me to spot and weed out the weeds, the lies, the dishonesty, pride and fear. And help me to watch over and care for those shoots of Loving-kindness, of Wisdom, of Humility, of Hope, of Faith and Trust in You and of Your Love, Your special Agape, selfless kind of love. And help me to grow my heart to steward more of You, Holy Spirit; to grow in maturity and favour with those around me, and especially with You, Lord[1].

Living and Breathing the Psalms

---

[1] Luke 2:52

Chapter 19 Covenant Partnership Responsibilities

With the tenderness of such an intimate and binding relationship, comes a weighty responsibility. From a distance, all that many see is the Lord's judgment. The ten commandments are clearly black and white. It is so easy to point to sin with its inevitable consequences of judgment. It requires an intimacy with Him to see the other side of His Character and Nature that He so longs for an excuse to bring Mercy instead. Many scriptures confirm His nature as One who shows Mercy, such as Romans 9:16 and 1 Peter 1:3, "Blessed be the God and Father of our Lord Jesus Christ, which according to his abundant mercy hath begotten us again unto a lively hope by the resurrection of Jesus Christ from the dead." Like a just judge in a courtroom when the case is clearly done and dusted, that judgment is deserved and the verdict is unequivocal. However much the judge may want to, he cannot give a merciful verdict unless an appropriate case can be made, or he would be unjust.

When we see sin, evil and injustice, does our heart cry out for justice? We have a mighty and weighty responsibility to see it for precisely what it is. We have a responsibility to feel the weight of the evil and injustice, its hurt and pain. But we have a responsibility to then to go into the Lord's Presence and from His Love transforming us, to make the case and plead for mercy.

From a distance, the evil, the hurt, the pain and loss that resulted from that evil, does not fully register in us. To those with hearts of love we can scarcely comprehend the hearts of those who plot evil and control, murder and thievery, mockery of our Saviour Jesus and the huge price that He paid to forgive us and adopt us into His family. But when we are up close and personal, when it directly affects us and those who we love, then it causes us to shout for justice. But we are called to go on from there and into that intimate place with Him, so that our heart is transformed to become like His, such that we long to bring Mercy in place of judgment. That's a very tough assignment. That requires a deep level of loving our enemies, forgiving and loving them while hating their sin. Mercy triumphs over justice, James 2:13.

This is the story of Stephen in Acts 6-7. He saw the evil of the accusers raised against him:

> Ye stiffnecked and uncircumcised in heart and ears, ye do always resist the Holy Ghost: as your father did, so do ye. Which of the prophets have not your fathers persecuted? And they have slain them which showed before of the coming of the Just One; of whom ye have been now the betrayers and murderers: who have received the law by the disposition of angels, and have not kept it. (KJV)
>
> Acts 7:51-53

But Stephen's response at the end was:

> He kneeled down, and cried with a loud voice, Lord, lay not this sin to their charge. And when he had said this, he fell asleep. (KJV)   Acts 7:60

The psalmist touches on this in Psalm 73. For the first 16 verses he is bewildered, frustrated and appalled by the evil of those around him with no sign of justice. But as he says in verse 17, when he went into the sanctuary and drew close to the Lord, he began to see the bigger picture, and describes it like waking from a dream. His soul was grieved and his heart pricked as he realized just how brutish and ignorant he had become while away from the presence of the Lord. (Verses 20-22.)

The Lord needs us to construct a case for Mercy to be shown, and shown to the very people whose evil has impacted us. If we had glimpsed the horrors of hell and the nature of eternal judgment then maybe like the psalmist we would find this easier to do. This is not easy nor does it come naturally. It doesn't! It only comes from imbibing our Daddy's sweet Nature and drinking of His sweet Spirit from spending time in His Presence. In His Presence, we appreciate something of how precious and sweet His transformation is to our hearts. In His Presence we learn how much we value and need that which has been so freely given to us, which we never deserved for a moment.

Abraham, Moses and David were put in this situation a number of times, especially Moses.

Some people have gone so far into evil that if shown Mercy it actually pushes them further into their sin. Evil has so distorted their understanding that showing them Mercy isn't seen as a good and helpful, but is seen as weakness. Judges face this all the time in their sentencing. The case will be made for mercy to be shown, but there is this secondary aspect to consider as well. Will a light sentence simply encourage the offender to continue their lawless ways or has due process brought them to their senses? As each plague hit, Pharaoh had a choice of how to react. He freely chose to harden his heart against the Lord, until it is as though he eventually stepped over a point of no return. From this point on the Lord was going to use Pharaoh's very hardness of heart to become an example for all time.

Exodus 9:7 says, "the heart of Pharaoh was stubborn and he did not let the people go." (ASV) But for the next plague of boils it says in vs 12, and "Jehovah hardened the heart of Pharaoh." (ASV) In the next plague, the plague of hail, Jehovah states clearly to Moses in verse 16, "but in very deed for this cause have I made thee to stand to show thee My Power, and that My Name may be declared throughout all the earth." (ASV)

So as situations develop that deserve judgment, will we step into this aspect of our role with the Lord, as our Heavenly Dad's Covenant Partner, and plead for Mercy in the middle of the evil? In order to do that, we need to ask the Lord to soften the hearts partnering with evil, so that they turn towards the Lord, in His Mercy, rather than become harder into their rebellion and go past that point of no return.

In Genesis 18:17-18 the Lord is questioning Himself over Abraham, as to whether or not, He will hide from Abraham what He purposed?

¹⁷ And the Lord said, Shall I hide from Abraham that thing which I do;

¹⁸ Seeing that Abraham shall surely become a great and mighty nation, and all of the nations of the earth shall be blessed in him? (KJV)

Is our relationship with Him such that He will be asking Himself the same questions over people and situations around us? Does He know that we will be pleading His Mercy, when the rampant evil clearly deserves His Judgment? When everything shouts, "Judgment is deserved and is irrevocable," and our insides revolt at the evil, what is our response?

When He gives you insight into the evil around you, how will you respond? Remember that Mercy, by its very definition, is never deserved.

Chapter 20 Your Covenant Partnership Role

A Covenant Partner has a number of different possible roles. So what's yours?

Remember that your responsibilities grow as you grow, so your role will likely change and develop as you grow in your relationship with your Heavenly Dad, your Covenant Partner.

Watchman on the wall	—warning
	—welcoming
Warrior	—pleading the Blood
	—prophetic declaration
Intercessor	—advocate in Heaven's Court
Apostle	—this is someone whose role is to bring heaven to earth. [So you need to know what Heaven looks like, first!]

This list is certainly not meant to be exhaustive, simply indicative of some of them. And these roles are not exclusive. You may be a watchman in the morning and need to be a warrior in the afternoon in a completely different situation.

And don't forget the vital part that Communion plays in fulfilling your role, whatever it is. Remember that this is a re-enactment of the Covenant inauguration at the Last Supper. This is your signing up to being a Covenant Partner with the All-Mighty-One. Remember that this is a two-way Covenant.

While there are responsibilities, don't lose sight of your own personal blessings, your dreams and their fulfilment. Each of us is unique, uniquely designed by a master craftsman to show off His Handiwork, and also to fulfil very unique and individual destinies.

> For He is a master craftsman, and we are His handiwork. We are displays of His workmanship. He created each one of us in Jesus our Messiah to uniquely display His Nature by the good, selfless paths He created a long time ago for each of us to walk.
>
> Ephesians 2:10   *L & B Translation*

You will often need to bring many aspects of your life and destiny to Him as you celebrate and partake of this Communion.

Being a Covenant Partner with the Lord, gives us great responsibilities for those around us, to plead their case before the Lord, on their behalf. The Lord shared His plans and purposes with Abraham, giving Abraham the responsibility to plead mercy on those otherwise set for judgment.

Moses' situation was very similar, with his repeatedly having to plead for the people, as I have outlined. He repeatedly pleaded their case at the complete expense of himself (Exodus 32:32).

It may at first glance seem that David was very different to Moses, but his reality is also very selfless. He didn't take on Goliath for his own glory. His biggest driving motivator was Goliath's taunting the Lord, his God and Covenant Partner. This makes for a different, and I believe correct, perspective on David's life. Remember it ends with him making huge, costly and extravagant preparations for building the temple, that he knew he would never see, but a place for giving His Covenant Partner honor and worship.

So are we equally selfless in our responsibilities? Are we pleading justice on our enemies or are we standing before our Covenant Partner pleading Mercy on them? Are we reasoning with the Lord as to why He should stay His hand from bringing judgment on them?

Are you secure in your relationship with the Lord? Have you developed an intimate relationship with Him? A relationship where you are fully exposed and open to Him, so that He *cannot* withhold what He plans unless, like Moses, you "reason with Him" Isaiah 1:18? Are you so exposed and open to Him that He can expose Himself to you? This is the intimacy to which you are called.

Last, but by no means least, are the Lord's Covenant Promises to bless you way beyond your wildest dreams:

> He delights to far exceed our wildest dreams or imaginings in the ways His power works in and through us to bring glory and honor to our Anointed Jesus through His Church. This will continue generation by generation forever.
> Ephesians 3:20-21   *L & B Translation*

This is not about your needs, but about your wants and dreams. This is to fulfil Jesus' promise that He came to give us life and life more abundantly, (John 10:10). He offers promises that will have you falling about laughing at their impossibility which He will fulfil to the letter if you can remain faithful and humble enough to steward them. That's much harder than you might think.

If your dreams are in fact your fulfilling His Dreams, you are in for a wild and crazy adventure. It took Samuel's mum a long time and much heartache until she finally voiced her longing to the Lord, only to find her dream dovetailed exactly into His. 1 Samuel 1 gives us the story of the barren wife of Elkanah who had two wives. Her husband's other wife provoked her sore, deliberately to aggravate her because she was barren and had no children. Evidently this had been going on for some time before she boiled over. On their annual visit to Shiloh where the Ark of the Covenant was, it says,

> she was in bitterness of soul, and prayed unto the Lord and wept sore. And she vowed a vow, and said, O Lord of hosts, if Thou wilt indeed look on the affliction of Thine Handmaid, and remember me, and not forget Thine Handmaid, but will give unto Thine Handmaid a man child, then I will give him unto the Lord all the days of his life. (KJV) 1 Samuel 1 10-11

This illustrates the real hidden stories behind Abraham, Moses and David.

If you are struggling with finding and understanding your destiny, you might try asking the Lord what He's dreaming for. Don't be surprised if this is far bigger than you could possibly achieve alone. But instead of shying away, simply ask yourself if you can steward it with Daddy's help. And remember, He thinks multi-generationally so also ask yourself if you can father the next generation to continue the mandate. With Daddy nothing is impossible (Luke 1:37) so...

Dream BIG!

Chapter 21   Seeming Impossibilities

I have a number of very special and highly valued unmarried friends, and couples who for one reason or another have not had children and are now well passed the age of childbearing. And so it is for you primarily, that I write this chapter, though there's much here for all of us.

You are NOT excluded from these wonderful, mighty and precious promises extending down the generations, impossible though that may sound. Our God delights in the impossible!

Isaiah gives a whole chapter to spell this out, just for you! "Sing, O barren, thou that didn't not bear; break forth into singing and cry aloud, though that didst not travail with child: for more are the children of the desolate than the children of the married wife, saith the Lord," Isaiah 54:1.

He is not just promising you can match your fruitful neighbour or friend, He is promising *more—a whole lot more*! While you are shaking your head, at this point, this is not my idea, these are not my words. Go back and re-read them for a moment and let that verse sink in. This is our Daddy's word, the All-Mighty-One's word specifically for you. Let that smile of incredulity spread across your face and yes, laugh loudly. Break out into singing.

Verse 2: In His Word to Isaiah He then spells out exactly what you are to do about it. But OK, you are going to have to believe this crazy promise in order to take these steps. "Enlarge the place of your tent, and let them stretch forth the curtains of thine habitations, spare not, lengthen thy cords and strengthen thy stakes;" In my language, "Take Him at His Word, and get building." As the Passion Translation® so aptly expresses it, "Increase is coming," so you had better prepare

119

for it, enlarge anything you can. "Enlarge your tent and add extensions to your dwelling. Hold nothing back!" Now is the very time to press on and build your ministry, and the work the Lord has called you to do.

Verse 3: So you have a choice to make. You can choose the route of Oh how miserable I am, "I have no children and no possibility of any legacy." Or you can choose to break out into praise, into worship and into thankfulness at what the Lord has given you to steward and to grow. And you can leave with Him just who He counts as your children. But rest assured that they, the very ones who have caught your vision, your anointing and your fire, will increase and break out everywhere, especially where He Himself is not known, where His Ways are not known, or where His Ways have been thrown out. There are desolate cities; cities that once prospered because of His ruling over them. There are cities that followed His rule of Justice and Peace, that have since gone to rack and ruin. As He puts it, these desolate cities will once more be re-built by your children bringing back His Rule and His Ways.

Verse 4: As always He gives us choices. Yes, these are often difficult, but they are for us to make and only we can make them. "Fear not, for you will not be ashamed." Yes, the shame of your youth, of all your mistakes or whatever, and much that may well have been way beyond you to control, all of this will be wiped out of your memory because of what your children carry and the number of them.

Verse 5: And to rub it in, He gives us a reminder of who He is. He is the very One who made us, and wants to be that intimate with us as the husband or wife you always dreamed of. And then to crown all of that He reminds us He is not just the romantic lover of our hearts, but He is a Mighty Warrior, the Lord of Heaven's Armies, and He is our Redeemer who laid down His Life as the payment for our redemption, and is now the God of the whole Earth, whose name is above every other name.

Verse 6: This is the One who is looking to take your hand in marriage. He recognises how you were forsaken and all it cost you. He recognises the hurt and grief you bore in your spirit.

Verse 7 & 8: So here is His very personal word specifically to you. "It may have looked like I also had forsaken you for a moment with all that you went through, but… But with *great* Mercy I will gather you with everlasting kindness." Verse 9 Regardless of how overwhelming the situation you are in right now, *this* great Mercy, and tender loving care, especially in My intimate sweet-talk to you, is My Covenant Promise to you from now on, just as I promised to Noah (so here the Lord is even underlining His Covenant Promise, Genesis 9:8-17).

It is those very points of hurt, grief and anguish that He is going to address, and speak His Promises right into.

Verse 10: Regardless of what appears ahead, regardless of how bad the situation looks, regardless of how impossible… My Kindness shall not depart, neither shall My Kindness and Peace that I have covenanted to you.

Verse 11 & 12: I will lay a beautiful rich foundation of royal blue for your work and beautify you and your work with precious and colourful gems.

Verse 13: "And *ALL* your children will be taught of the Lord and great shall be the peace of your children." But hold on a minute, this whole chapter is written to those who have no children. Oh Yes, they are coming!

Verse 14: But not just your children will know deep peace, but you too will be far from the very things that haunted your past, oppression, fear and terror.

Verse 15 & 16: All of those plots hatched against you will fall and all of their expensive and costly warmongering against you will amount to absolutely nothing.

And I so love this final verse:

Verse 17: No weapon that is formed against thee shall prosper; and every tongue that shall rise against thee in judgment though shalt condemn. This is the heritage of the servants of the Lord, and their righteousness is of Me, saith the Lord.

This is YOUR heritage. Married or not, with natural children or not, this is your heritage. This is our Heavenly Daddy's heart and longing for each one of us. This isn't by anything you are doing, or can do to earn it, but the love that Jesus demonstrated in His Life and through His Death and Resurrection.

As Paul set out for us in Romans 4:5
If you think you can earn that right standing with Father God you will be always working. But for those who instead simply believe His Word, find that they are indeed forgiven and made right with Father God, through the blood of Jesus—not by anything that they have done to earn it.

L & B Translation

You are His Bride. The Song of Songs paints something of Jesus' longing heart for you and me, as His Bride. Something of this has been wonderfully captured by Carolyn Billing in her song 'Jesus Singing to the Bride (You have ravished My Heart) Song of Songs 4:7-15 (TPT)'.

Working through this chapter has been difficult for me. The Lord's promises are too big, too outrageous, too unreal. His promises to me feel that way, which is why I dare not mention them, other than to say that Covenant is one small key in there. They are way past my own experience of Him thus far. But they were way past those biblical characters too, to whom they were directly given.

I'm hardly the first to say this, but if the Lord's promises to you don't have you falling about laughing at their absurdity, then they are probably not His promises to you. His promises are completely outrageous, so what will you do with them, and how will you steward them? Most of us probably ignore them as fantasy dreaming, completely missing who originated the very idea of them, deep in our hearts and spirits. Such is our unbelief. Let's face it, for this is what it is.

As our Heavenly Daddy, He wants the very best for us, but on His Terms. I'm rather concluding He enjoys having us laughing so. He never criticized Sarah or Abraham for their laughter, though He did like to remind them of it, "Nay; but though didst laugh," Genesis 18:15 (KJV).

Are you catching His drift here? We really shouldn't be surprised by the beginning of Psalm 100 which says, "Make a joyful shout to the Lord..." for this is the roadmap into the Lord's Presence, He likes joyful company, just like we do! And He delights to take that point of our deepest pain, hurt, or longing and turn it totally on its head. These 'way out there promises' touch precisely those deep places in our hearts and lives, just as they did for Abraham, Moses and David.

Will we laugh until our faith has caught up with His reality and promise to us? That's a tough one. It's brutal, but highly effective, to look at the Lord's very personal Promises to us and laugh with them. As they touch points of our deepest hurt and pain it becomes doubly difficult. Can you look at your Heavenly Daddy and see His questioning look? Will you laugh with Him and see the smile stretch across His Face? This is a direct effort of your spirit, probably dragging your will kicking and screaming behind you. I never said it was easy, and neither did He.

I struggle with thinking of what I need to do to bring about what He has promised, and that's painful! But these promises have nothing to do with what *we* can bring about—that's rather the point! He's the one who will do it, and He will do it His Way. This is freeing—this takes the weight off me and begins to release the smile, and eventually the laughter, back to Him. All He asks is for our cooperation and our willingness to say 'Yes!'

Maybe you are thinking that you haven't got any personal promises to start laughing over. Maybe... but have you dismissed promises He gave you months or years ago precisely because they were just too outrageous and unbelievable? Maybe you have to go back and ask Him to remind you, or to speak fresh promises, direct from His Heart to yours. Stop for a moment and listen to just what daydreams are springing up as you read this.

So where do you start? Right where you are. One of the difficulties is seeing the richness of where we are; of seeing the oak tree in the acorn sitting in the palm of our hand. An oak tree looks nothing like an acorn! There are also serious contradictions in how the Lord does things. If you want to lead, then learn to serve. Joshua learned and earned his position to pick up the leadership from Moses, through serving Moses and understudying him. Elisha qualified for his ministry and double-portion anointing through serving Elijah. The principle still applies today, with Benny Hinn serving Kathryn Kuhlman with her evangelistic and healing ministry,

Kenneth Copeland being a pilot for Oral Roberts and learning to minister alongside him, and Daniel Kolenda serving the evangelist Reinhard Bonnke, as some high profile examples.

Look to those who you respect, and choose to honor them and the anointing they carry [period!]. Choose ways to serve them, not for how you can gain, but simply out of a heart to serve. With today's social media it is very easy to follow someone, even from another country. Will you encourage them? Will you defend them when those around you criticise or trample that person's ideas or position? And considerably more difficult, will you defend them in the spirit of love, freedom and joy, respecting others who choose to see things differently. Remember that those critics will be the ones who are missing out. Those critics are the ones who will be missing out on the life, the wisdom and the anointing that the Lord longs to freely lavish on us all.

Let's remember that when the nations are raging against the Lord and taking counsel together against Him, Psalm 2:4 reminds us that 'He who sits in the heavens is laughing at them, mocking them.' I think Elijah was in that place on Mount Carmel as he mocked the prophets of Baal in 1 Kings 18:27. The polite version from the (KJV) reads "Cry aloud: for he is a god; either he is talking, or he is pursuing, or he is on a journey, or peradventure he sleepeth, and must be awaked." I think the truth was probably closer to, "You'll have to shout a tad louder, He's God after all! Hah, maybe he's too deep in contemplation, or perhaps he's relieving himself, or off some-place else on holiday. He's probably sleeping; try a bit louder and wake him up!"

Psalm 16:11 "You will reveal to me the pathway of life, for in Your Presence is the very fullness of JOY!" (The author's own rendering.) For myself, I have drunk the pain and sorrow of His Compassion, but only very rarely have I even glimpsed at His Fullness of JOY. And yet Joy, and not compassion, is one third of the Kingdom, equal together with Love and Peace, Galatians 5:22.

I am sure you can readily complete this page with people who had no natural heirs, but have many sons and daughters who fulfil the Lord's Isaiah 54 promise to them. For starters I give you Mother Teresa, Derek & Lydia Prince and Corrie ten Boom...

Postscript

I have just been enjoying Johnny Enlow's talk on Elijah Streams, entitled "Pastoring the Prophetic" from 24ᵗʰ Jan 2022. https://www.elijahstreams.com/watch/watch.php?ID=964
35 minutes in from the start he unpacks Psalm 100 and gives specific steps, as the pathway into that secret place with the Lord:

Verse 1.   Make a *Joyful shout* to the Lord (all ye lands)

Verse 2.   Serve the Lord with gladness:
Come before *His Presence* with singing.

His Presence we can find on our own.

Come with singing.

Verse 3.1. Know ye that the Lord He is God: it is He that hath made us, and not we ourselves; we are *His People*, He is God and we are *His People*.

He has a family for you.

Meditate on His Lordship

Verse 3.2. We are the sheep of *His Pasture.*
He has a place for you and in *His Pasture* there's an assignment for you.

We belong to Him—we have been bought with a price.

Next we are stepping through into a place with limited access:
Verse 4.1 Enter through *His Gates* with thanksgiving.
Thanksgiving reminds you of what He's done in the past, and in your past, and what He's doing in your present

Come with Thanksgiving

With thanks on your lips and a thankful heart.

Verse 4.2. Enter *His Courts* with Praise.
Come with Praise.

Allow your thanks to move to Praise.

Praise Him for all you know and have experienced Him to be for you.

Verse 4.3. Bless *His Name.*
His Names express facets of who He is, so move your Praise to
High Praise of all of His many names…

And to High Praise of all who He is,
regardless of whether He has been that for you.

Especially praise Him for what His Word says He is that you haven't yet experienced, but need right now.

Verse 5.1 For the Lord is Good, *His Mercy* endures forever.
Come Boldy

Pour out your heart—He is Good.

Verse 5.2. *His Truth* endures to all generations.
Listen as He shares 'His truth' with you; this often violates facts.

And I would like to add here,

then laugh,

laugh

and laugh some more!

He *is* faithful who promised. Hebrews 10:23

So let us hold fast to the confession of our faith and our hope in Him, for the very one who promised this to us, is forever absolutely faithful.   Hebrews 10:23
L & B Translation

A study guide to accompany this book is now available,

Covenant Partnership
    Study-Guide Workbook

This Bible-Study Workbook accompanies *Covenant Partnership – Beyond the Courts of Heaven*. It is designed for individual or group study and as a notebook for recording your discussions, thoughts, and dreams. It will help you work through, take to heart and drive deep into your spirit the truths of the Partnership with the Lord to which we are called as outlined here in *Covenant Partnership*.

If you have been impacted and encouraged by this book, and find it helpful, I ask that that you recommend it to others. For that, there's a very vital part you can play. Please go back and leave a review on Amazon. This is a very key part of passing the message on, as well of course recommending it to your friends. Your reviews count very strongly to people evaluating whether a particular book is worth reading.

Thank you so much.

If you would like to get in touch with the author, then please visit www.landbreathingt.com. If you subscribe then you will be kept abreast of the work on other books, and blog updates as the work progresses.

About the Author

Jim Edwards is a passionate lover of Jesus. He lives on the South Coast of the UK. He has four amazing and wonderful children, and two grandchildren.

Now retired and full-time writer, he was Technical Sales Manager for a high voltage power supply company. This required regular visits to his USA customers enabling him to go on to Bethel Church in Redding, California. The role was to explain the details of the electronics to technical and non-technical people alike. Now remember that you cannot see electrons, so the role translated to that of explaining the operation and details of things that you cannot see to a wide variety of people.

His hope and prayer is that you have repeatedly encountered Father, Jesus, and Holy Spirit through this book and found them to be drawing you closer in their wondrous love. Our One True God loves you dearly and longs to bless you outrageously. Jim would always love to hear the story of your encounters and how they have impacted your life. He can be contacted via www.landbreathingt.com the Edwards Family website, or Edwards Family Publishing on Facebook.

This is the seventh of a number of books, this being the sequel to *Mercy—God's Covenant Assistance*. There are more books to follow—watch this space.

Additional Books by the Author:
[All available from Amazon]

Covenant Partnership
Study-Guide Workbook

This Bible-Study Workbook accompanies *Covenant Partnership – Beyond the Courts of Heaven*. It is designed for individual or group study and as a notebook for recording your discussions, thoughts, and dreams. It will help you work through, take to heart and drive deep into your spirit the truths of the Partnership with the Lord to which we are called as outlined in Covenant Partnership.

Jesus cut covenant with His Father on our behalf, to make a deep loving relationship with God, the All-Mighty-One, available to you and I.

This powerful dimension to your relationship with Father God builds on the legal frameworks of the Courts of Heaven and Blood Covenant. Through our New Covenant with Jesus, we are brought into this intimate, trusting relationship with our Heavenly Father who is longing to open up and reveal His Heart to you.

Covenant Partnership is explored through the lives of Abraham, Moses and David who illustrate the intimacy, responsibility and the huge blessing our Heavenly Father has for each one of us.

Far greater than you dared to imagine, your destiny spans the generations and is promised to you with all the power of His legally binding blood covenant. Are you hungry enough to search out His Ways and His Plans for you and your children's children down the generations?

This is your assignment.

Edwards Family Publishing:
    ISBN-13:   9798854423007
    ISBN-10:
    Kindle ASIN: Not yet available

COVENANT
PARTNERSHIP

Study-Guide

Workbook

Jim Edwards

Mercy—God's Mighty Covenanted Assistance for You.

Mercy is covenant assistance, and its roots tell us a lot about the nature and character of our Heavenly Father, and His commitment to His covenants.

God is a God of Covenant, so this book illustrates and explains what a 'blood covenant' actually is and compares and contrasts the different covenants God has made, and why He makes them.

God has repeatedly bound Himself with covenants. Why? Because He wants to bless people outrageously. Would you like to be included?

Jesus cut a very binding 'blood covenant' with His Father, on our behalf, at the cross. This book spells out just what is included for you and me and how we are to draw on it.

Edwards Family Publishing: Print & Kindle
ISBN—13: 978-1523342068
ISBN—10: 15323342064
ASIN: B01LWBKJRC

MERCY

GOD'S
COVENANT
ASSISTANCE

Jim Edwards

Your Invitation

Now where should a Passion Play end?

Good Friday is over and the tomb closed and sealed.

Eavesdrop on a group whose play doesn't end where their scriptwriter intended.

Join them for their Easter service, and travel with them, as they experience for themselves the resurrection appearances of Jesus.

Did Jesus really rise from the dead? Does it matter? Is it of any relevance for us? How would you recognize Him? What would it look like, if He were to come back today? How could He help you?

Then share in their very personal invitation to a life—changing encounter.

This is Your Invitation.

Edwards Family Publishing:
ISBN—10: 1497403081
ISBN—13: 978-1497403086
ASIN: B00BTNGYM0

Living and Breathing the Psalms

Living and Breathing the Psalms is a raw and very personal prayer journey.

Here are the Old Covenant prayers, poems and songs to the Lord, reframed through intimacy and relationship with each member of the Trinity. From this perspective the Psalms break open in a simple, fresh and dynamic way.

Key life themes lie in these ancient songs of worship, at the very heart of Old Covenant experience, belief and ritual. Exploring them, we find them unlocked through an intimate relationship with our Saviour and King, Firstborn Son of our Heavenly Papa God, as revealed to us by Holy Spirit.

Here, unashamedly viewed through faith and trust in Mighty King Jesus, Mashiach, the Anointed One, is pain, hurt and grief, side by side with fire, passion, love, thanks, praise and worship.

As you put your trust, hope and faith in Him, may you find here your heart's cries to our High King of Heaven and Earth.

Available from Amazon   Print & Kindle
ISBN—13: 978-1535590730
ISBN—10: 1535590734
ASIN: B01LOZL5MQ

Living and Breathing Romans to Galatians

Living and Breathing Romans to Galatians is an easy reading paraphrase of the Epistles. Here are Paul's early letters to these embryonic early churches.

Guarded, and carefully copied through the centuries for us, they are now unravelled in a fresh way, in the everyday language of today. They are here amplified to explain the revelation Paul personally received from Jesus that he was so concerned to share with all who would receive it. Here is Paul's heart revealed, alongside the price he paid to share this Good News of Jesus.

Here is the Good News that the same Holy Spirit who anointed Jesus wants to live in you, to strengthen you and demonstrate with signs and wonders through you that Jesus is our Redeemer and Father God's Anointed Son.

The reality of the promises, the prayers and the truths of this wonderful Good News that Jesus paid such a high price to bring us, is vibrantly brought to life. While Holy Spirit's life-changing, heart-changing, healing power to comfort, to save, to deliver, to restore, and to bring hope is here laid out for us.

Alongside the text, are thought provoking study questions, notes and cross references, to unveil the enormity of all that Jesus won for us, and to reveal our Heavenly Father's wondrous heart of love; His longing to know and be known, by us all.

Available from Amazon   Print & Kindle
ISBN-13: 978-1727130621
ISBN-10: 1727139626
Kindle ASIN: B08WJ8ZYKY
This is the companion volume to Living and Breathing Hebrews to Jude, and Living and Breathing Ephesians to
    Philemon.

Living and Breathing Ephesians to Philemon

Living and Breathing Ephesians to Philemon is an easy reading paraphrase of these Epistles. Here are Paul's letters to these embryonic early churches; many written from prison, and a couple shortly before he was martyred.

Guarded, and carefully copied through the centuries for us, they are now unravelled in a fresh way, in the everyday language of the twenty-first century. They are here amplified to explain the revelation Paul personally received from Jesus that he was so concerned to share with all who would receive it.

Here is Paul's heart revealed, with his instructions and encouragement to his closest friends and co-workers. Here are his descriptions of a life Anointed by Holy Spirit who wants to live in us, to strengthen you and I to demonstrate with signs and wonders through us that Jesus is our Redeemer and Father God's Anointed Son, and Lord of All.

The reality of the promises, the prayers and the truths of this wonderful Good News that Jesus paid such a high price to bring us, is vibrantly brought to life. While Holy Spirit's anointing, to bring life-changing, heart-changing, healing power to comfort, to save, to deliver, to restore, and to bring hope is here laid out.

Alongside the text, are thought provoking study questions, notes and cross references, to unveil the enormity of all that Jesus won for us, to reveal our Heavenly Father's wondrous heart of love; His longing to know and be known, by us all.

Available from Amazon   Print & Kindle

ISBN-13: 9781704705958

ISBN-10: 1704705959

Kindle ASIN: B08WPYZ3K2

This is the companion volume to *Living and Breathing Romans to Galatians* and *Living and Breathing Hebrews to Jude*.

Covenant Partnership

Living and Breathing Hebrews to Jude

Living and Breathing Hebrews to Jude is an easy reading paraphrase of the Epistles. Here are letters written to us from those who knew Jesus intimately, who were brought up with Him, or spent years with Him as His disciples.

Guarded, and carefully copied through the centuries for us, they are now unravelled in a fresh way, in the everyday language of today. They are here amplified to explain the truths those early followers of Jesus were so concerned to pass on to their fellow believers.

The reality of the promises, the prayers and the truths of the wonderful good news that Jesus paid such a high price to bring us, is vibrantly brought to life. While Holy Spirit's life—changing, heart—changing, healing power to comfort, to save, to deliver, to restore, and to bring hope—is here laid out for us.

Alongside the text are thought-provoking study questions, notes and cross references, to unveil the enormity of all that Jesus won for us, and to reveal our Heavenly Father's wondrous heart of love; His longing to know and be known, by us all.

Available from Amazon   Print & Kindle
ISBN—13: 978-1979871358
ISBN—10: 1979871353
Kindle ASIN:B08VW9G9ZT

This is the companion volume to *Living and Breathing Romans to Galatians* and *Living and Breathing Ephesians to Philemon.*

Living & Breathing Hebrews to Jude

Jim Edwards

Made in the USA
Middletown, DE
02 September 2024